THE UNDO PRINCIPLE

The Backwards Approach That Actually Works

by Sofia Winters

THE UNDO PRINCIPLE
The Backwards Approach That Actually Works

First Edition: December 2025

ISBN: 979-8-90271-712-6

Publisher's Disclaimer:
This book is designed to provide helpful information on the subjects discussed. It is sold with the understanding that the publisher and author are not engaged in rendering psychological, medical, legal, or other professional services. If expert assistance is required, the services of a competent professional should be sought.

The author and publisher specifically disclaim any liability, loss, or risk, personal or otherwise, that is incurred as a consequence, directly or indirectly, of the use and application of any of the contents of this book.

Some names and identifying details have been changed to protect the privacy of individuals.

Printed in the United States of America

For my grandmother,

who answered the phone at 2 AM

and taught me that letting go

is not the same as giving up.

Your wisdom in that parking lot conversation

didn't just change my life,

it became this book.

Contents

INTRODUCTION: The Night I Realized I Was Doing Everything Wrong

I was sitting in my parked car at 2 AM, mascara running down my face, sobbing so hard I could barely catch my breath.

Not because something terrible had happened. Not because I'd lost someone I loved or faced some devastating crisis. I was crying because I had everything I thought I wanted, and I was absolutely miserable.

The promotion I'd manifested. The relationship I'd visualized. The apartment I'd scripted into existence with perfect present-tense affirmations. All of it was real. All of it was mine. And I felt more trapped than I'd ever felt in my life.

The Poster Child for Manifestation

For three years, I had been the walking, talking embodiment of everything the manifestation world teaches you to do.

My bedroom walls were covered in vision boards, so many that you could barely see the paint underneath. Images of successful women in corner offices, couples laughing on beaches, designer handbags, meditation retreats in Bali. I'd cut them out with such precision, arranged them with such intention, visualized myself into each scenario until

I could practically feel the sand between my toes and smell the ocean air.

Every morning, I woke up at 5:30 AM, no matter how exhausted I was, to journal in present tense about my dream life as if it had already happened. "I am so grateful for my six-figure income. I am so blessed to be in a loving, committed relationship with my soulmate. I am living in my dream apartment in the perfect neighborhood." I wrote these sentences over and over, filling page after page, trying to convince the universe (and myself) that these things were already mine.

I meditated twice a day, following guided visualizations that instructed me to "feel the feelings" of having what I wanted. I listened to subliminal affirmations while I slept. I set intentions during every new moon and released what wasn't serving me during every full moon. I drank moon water. I carried crystals. I burned sage. I did everything.

I read every book. I followed every guru. I bought every course that promised to teach me the "real secret" to getting what I wanted. I knew about vibrations and frequencies. I understood the law of attraction. I could quote Neville Goddard and Abraham Hicks. I was fluent in the language of manifestation.

And it worked. Sort of.

When Your Manifestations Show Up Wrong

The promotion came through exactly when I'd visualized it would, right before my 30th birthday, just like I'd written in my journal a hundred times. I got the title, the salary bump, the corner office with windows overlooking the city. I'd manifested it down to the smallest detail.

What I hadn't manifested, what nobody tells you to visualize, was the boss who would make every day feel like walking on eggshells. The way she'd question my worth in subtle, cutting ways that made me doubt every decision. The Sunday night anxiety that became so familiar I could taste it. The way I'd sit in that corner office with those perfect windows and feel like I was suffocating.

The relationship manifested too. I met him at a coffee shop, exactly like I'd visualized. He checked every box on my list: kind, successful, good-looking, shared my values, wanted the same things in life. On paper, he was perfect.

In reality? He made me feel small. Not through anything obvious, he never yelled or criticized directly. But there was this constant undertone of disappointment, like I was never quite measuring up to what he'd hoped I'd be. I found myself editing my personality, dimming my light, shrinking myself to fit into the vision I'd created. The version of me in the relationship wasn't actually me at all.

And the apartment. God, the apartment. It was beautiful, exposed brick, natural light, in the neighborhood I'd circled on my vision board map. It was also so expensive that I had no money left over for anything else. No money to actually enjoy the city I'd been so desperate to live in. No money to travel, to try new restaurants, to take the pottery class I'd always wanted to take. I was living in my dream apartment, working at my dream job, dating my dream guy, and I couldn't afford to have a life.

The Moment It All Collapsed

That night in the car, I'd just come from dinner with my boyfriend. We'd gone to this trendy restaurant I could barely afford, where I'd ordered the cheapest thing on the menu and pretended I wasn't stressed about it. He'd spent most of the dinner checking his phone and making comments about how I should probably start going to the gym more if I wanted to "maintain my appearance."

I smiled through it. I'd become so good at smiling through it.

On the drive home, he told me he thought I was "too sensitive" when I mentioned that his comment had hurt my feelings. "I'm just trying to help you be your best self," he said. "Isn't that what you're always talking about? Becoming your highest version?"

And something inside me just... broke.

I dropped him off, drove three blocks, pulled into a random parking lot, and completely fell apart.

Because he was right. This was what I'd been talking about. Becoming my highest version. Manifesting my dream life. Creating the reality I desired.

So why did my "dream life" feel like a nightmare?

The Conversation That Changed Everything

Through my tears, I called my grandmother. It was 2 AM, but she answered on the second ring like she'd been waiting for my call.

"Mija," she said, her voice thick with sleep and concern. "What's wrong?"

I tried to explain through my sobs. The manifestation. The vision boards. The affirmations. How I'd done everything right and it all felt so wrong.

"Tell me about this life you manifested," she said gently.

So I did. I told her about the job, the boyfriend, the apartment. I told her about my morning routine, my meditation practice, my journals full of affirmations. I told her about how hard I was working to hold onto it all, to keep vibrating at the right frequency, to stay positive enough to maintain everything I'd created.

There was a long pause on the other end of the line.

"Mija," she finally said, "you sound exhausted."

"Well, yes," I said, a bit defensively. "Manifestation takes work. You have to stay consistent, stay in the vibration, keep, "

"No, my love. You sound exhausted from trying to convince yourself you're happy."

The words hit me like a physical blow.

"You just described a job that makes you anxious, a man who makes you feel small, and an apartment you can't afford," she continued, her voice impossibly tender. "Are you sure you manifested what you wanted, or what you thought you were supposed to want?"

I couldn't answer. I couldn't even breathe.

"And another thing," she said. "All this 'holding on' you're doing, the affirmations, the visualizations, the trying to stay in the right vibration. Doesn't it seem like maybe you're clutching these things so tight because you're afraid they'll disappear if you relax for even a second?"

She was right. God, she was so right.

Every morning, I woke up with a knot of anxiety in my stomach, terrified that if I didn't do my affirmations perfectly, if I didn't visualize hard enough, if I let my vibration drop for even a moment, everything would crumble.

I wasn't living. I was white-knuckling my way through a life I'd built with a very detailed blueprint but no actual connection to what I truly wanted.

The Question That Started Everything

"What if," my grandmother said slowly, "you've been doing this backwards?"

"What do you mean?"

"What if all this trying, all this forcing, all this clutching and controlling and working so hard to make things happen... what if that's actually pushing away what you really want?"

I sat in that dark parking lot, phone pressed to my ear, and felt something shift inside me. Not a dramatic, lightning-bolt kind of shift. More like a whisper I'd been ignoring for months finally got loud enough to hear.

What if I've been doing this backwards?

What if the very act of holding on so tightly was cutting off my circulation? What if my grip on what I thought I wanted was preventing me from receiving what I actually needed?

I thought about holding sand. When you make a fist and try to clutch it tight, it pours out through the cracks between your fingers. But when you hold it with an open palm, you can hold more than you ever could by trying to control it.

"So what do I do?" I asked, my voice small.

"Maybe," she said, "you start by letting go."

The Beginning of the Undo

The next morning, I did something I hadn't done in three years.

Nothing.

I didn't journal. I didn't visualize. I didn't affirm or meditate or check my vision board. I didn't force myself to "feel the feelings" of my manifestations. I just... sat there.

And in that space of not-doing, I felt something I hadn't felt in years: relief.

It was subtle. Like taking off shoes that were half a size too small, you don't realize how much they hurt until they're off.

That relief scared me at first. My manifestation-trained mind immediately panicked. "What are you doing? You're going to lose everything! You have to stay in the vibration! You have to hold onto what you created!"

But underneath that panic was something else. Something quieter but infinitely more powerful: the recognition that I'd been exhausted for so long that I'd forgotten what it felt like to simply be.

The Experiment Begins

I decided to run an experiment. Just for two weeks, I told myself. Two weeks of not trying to control everything. Two weeks of releasing the death grip I had on my manifestations.

I took down one vision board. Then another. I stopped forcing myself to journal affirmations that felt like lies. I quit the manifestation course I'd been white-knuckling my way through, the one that cost $2,000 and promised to unlock my "quantum manifestation abilities."

I unfollowed the Instagram accounts that made me feel like I wasn't doing enough, being enough, vibrating high enough. The ones where perfect-looking people in perfect houses talked about their perfect manifestation practices and made me feel like a failure every time I scrolled past them.

And something strange happened.

Nothing fell apart.

In fact, things started to get... lighter.

The First Release

Two weeks into my experiment, I was sitting in my boss's office, and she said something particularly cutting about a project I'd been working on. The old me, the me from just weeks before, would have smiled, nodded, and immediately gone into overdrive trying to fix it, prove myself, work harder.

But something was different now. I'd stopped clutching so tightly to the manifestation of "perfect employee in perfect job." And in the space that opened up, I could finally see clearly:

This job was draining my soul.

Not because I wasn't working hard enough or vibrating high enough or visualizing well enough. Simply because it wasn't right for me. The promotion I'd manifested was a beautiful office I was supposed to want, not one I actually wanted.

And for the first time in years, I thought: "What if I just... quit?"

The old me would have been horrified. "You can't quit! You manifested this! You have to hold onto it! What about your vision board?"

But the new me, the me who was learning to release, thought: "What if holding on to this is harder than letting it go?"

I gave my notice the next day.

People thought I was having a breakdown. "What about your manifestation?" they asked. "Aren't you giving up on your dream?"

But I wasn't giving up. I was letting go. And there's a massive difference.

Giving Up vs. Letting Go

Giving up is collapse. Letting go is release.

Giving up says, "I can't do this anymore." Letting go says, "I don't have to control this anymore."

Giving up is passive defeat. Letting go is active trust.

Giving up happens when you're exhausted from trying to force something that isn't working. Letting go happens when you realize that the trying itself is the problem.

When I quit that job, I wasn't giving up on success or abundance or my career. I was letting go of my attachment to what that success "had" to look like. I was releasing my grip on a specific outcome that I'd convinced myself was the only acceptable path.

And in the space that opened up, something new could finally enter.

The Domino Effect

A month after quitting, I ended the relationship.

This was harder. I'd invested so much in manifesting "the perfect partner." I'd visualized him so specifically. I'd journaled about him for two years before we even met.

Walking away from him felt like walking away from years of manifestation work.

But I couldn't ignore the truth anymore: the relationship that looked perfect on paper felt wrong in my body.

Every time I was with him, my shoulders tensed up. My stomach knotted. My jaw clenched. My body had been screaming at me for months, but I'd been too busy trying to hold onto my manifestation to listen.

When I told him I wanted to end things, he said, "But we're perfect together. Everyone says so."

And that was the problem, wasn't it? We were perfect on paper. Perfect in theory. Perfect according to the checklist I'd made when I was visualizing my ideal partner.

But perfect on paper and right in reality are two completely different things.

I let him go.

Six weeks after that, I moved out of the expensive apartment and into a smaller place that actually felt like home. A place I could afford. A place where I could breathe.

What I Discovered in the Space

Over the next year, I became obsessed with understanding why letting go worked better than holding on.

I read everything I could find on attachment theory, neuroscience, energy psychology, and ancient spiritual practices. I interviewed people who had "manifested" incredible things, not through force, but through release. I studied the psychology of control and the physiology of stress. I experimented on myself relentlessly, testing every theory and tracking every result.

What I found changed everything I thought I knew about manifestation, success, and getting what you want in life.

The research was clear: our nervous systems literally cannot attract when they're in survival mode.

When we're gripping, controlling, desperately trying to force outcomes, we're sending our bodies the signal that we're unsafe. And an unsafe nervous system is a closed system. It can't receive. It can only defend.

Think about it: when you're clutching something with a death grip, can you receive anything else? When both hands are full, white-knuckled and trembling from the effort of holding on, how can anything new come to you?

But when we release? When we let go of the death grip on how things "have to" be?

That's when we become magnetic. That's when we create space for something better than we could have imagined to enter.

The Universal Truth I'd Missed

As I dove deeper into my research, I realized that every spiritual tradition throughout history taught some version of this principle:

Buddhism calls it non-attachment. The idea that suffering comes from clinging to things, people, and outcomes. That peace comes from holding things lightly.

Taoism calls it wu wei, effortless action. Going with the flow instead of against it. Acting in harmony with the natural way of things rather than trying to force reality to bend to your will.

Christianity talks about surrendering to God's plan. Letting go and letting God. Trusting that there's a wisdom greater than your own personal agenda.

Modern psychology calls it outcome independence. The ability to want something, work toward it, but not need it so desperately that you sabotage yourself in the pursuit.

They all pointed to the same fundamental truth: the tighter you hold, the more you lose.

And yet, somehow, the modern manifestation movement had missed this entirely. Or worse, twisted it into its opposite.

We'd been taught to hold tighter, visualize harder, affirm more frequently, control more precisely. We'd been taught that manifesting was about exerting our will on the universe, bending reality to our desires through sheer force of intention.

No wonder we were all exhausted.

The Paradox That Changes Everything

Here's what I learned, and what this book is really about:

You have to want it without needing it.

You have to hold the vision without clutching the outcome.

You have to care deeply while staying unattached to how it unfolds.

This isn't about being passive. It's not about giving up on your dreams or settling for less than you deserve. It's not about pretending you don't care or adopting some false sense of spiritual superiority where you claim to be "above" wanting things.

It's about understanding that your grip is the thing blocking your receiving.

Your white-knuckled control is the dam preventing the flow.

Your desperate need to make it happen exactly as you've planned is the wall between you and what's trying to reach you.

When I finally understood this, I mean really understood it, not just intellectually but in my bones, everything changed.

What This Book Will Teach You

In the pages ahead, I'm going to share everything I learned during my journey from exhausted manifestation addict to someone who actually receives what she wants by releasing the need to control how it comes.

You're going to learn the science behind why release creates attraction and why forcing creates resistance. You'll understand exactly what's happening in your nervous system when you're clutching versus when you're allowing.

You'll discover the exact moment you're blocking your own manifestations, and it's not when you think it is. You'll learn the difference between surrender and giving up, between trusting and being passive, between letting go and letting yourself down.

I'll show you the practical tools I developed for releasing without losing desire. The specific practices that help you want something powerfully while holding it lightly. The daily rituals that keep you in a state of allowing instead of forcing.

You'll hear stories from other people who manifested more by doing less. Who found love when they stopped chasing it, who created abundance when they stopped clutching their money, who healed their bodies when they stopped trying to control every symptom.

And most importantly, you'll learn how to apply this to your specific life: your relationships, your money, your career, your health, your purpose.

Who This Book Is For

This book is for you if:

You've done "all the manifestation things" but feel more exhausted than abundant. You're tired of vision boards that don't seem to work and affirmations that feel like lies you're telling yourself.

You're tired of white-knuckling your way through your spiritual practice, trying to force yourself to feel grateful when you actually feel frustrated, trying to "stay in the vibration" when you're exhausted and overwhelmed.

You've manifested things that looked good but felt wrong. Things that checked all the boxes on paper but left you feeling empty. Success that somehow felt like failure.

You're afraid that if you stop trying so hard, everything will fall apart. That the only thing holding your life together is your constant vigilance, your relentless effort, your refusal to relax for even a moment.

You're ready to discover what happens when you release the rope you've been pulling on. When you stop trying to force the river to flow uphill. When you finally, finally allow yourself to receive instead of constantly chasing.

This book is for the over-achievers who are tired of achieving. The control enthusiasts who are exhausted from controlling. The manifestation devotees who are ready to try something completely different.

This book is for anyone who's ever felt like they're doing everything "right" but still feeling utterly wrong.

What Makes This Different

This isn't another "10 steps to manifest your dream life" book. Those books are what got you here, exhausted, overwhelmed, and wondering why you're working so hard for results that feel hollow.

This is the book for what comes after. After you realize that more effort isn't the answer. After you understand that trying harder is actually making things harder. After you're ready to explore the possibility that the backwards approach might actually be the one that works.

I'm not going to tell you to create more vision boards or add more affirmations to your morning routine. I'm not going to give you a complicated manifestation formula or teach you how to "hack the universe."

Instead, I'm going to show you how to subtract. How to release. How to undo the gripping and grasping that's been exhausting you and blocking your blessings.

This is about subtraction, not addition. Space, not stuff. Releasing, not accumulating.

My Promise to You

I promise this book won't add more to your plate. It won't give you seventeen new practices to white-knuckle your way through or make you feel guilty for not trying hard enough.

If you're exhausted from trying so hard, this book will teach you how to attract by allowing.

If you're terrified of letting go, this book will show you that release is safety, not surrender, that holding on so tight is actually what's making you feel so precarious.

If you've forgotten what it feels like to simply be instead of constantly becoming, this book will help you remember.

The irony of manifestation, the thing nobody tells you, is that the moment you stop chasing is often the moment everything you wanted starts chasing you.

How to Use This Book

You can read this straight through, or jump to the chapters that call to you. Each part builds on the one before it, but they're also designed to stand alone.

If you're drowning in relationship anxiety, go straight to Part Ten. If money stress is crushing you, Part Nine will meet you where you are. If you're struggling with your health, Part Twelve was written for you.

At the end of each chapter, you'll find practical exercises and reflection questions. These aren't homework, they're invitations. Do them if they resonate. Skip them if they don't.

This book is about undoing, remember? You don't have to do everything "right."

In fact, that's exactly the mindset we're releasing.

Are You Ready?

That night in my car, sobbing at 2 AM, I thought I'd hit rock bottom.

Now I understand: I hadn't hit bottom. I'd hit a wall. The wall I'd built by trying so hard to control everything, by clutching so tightly to outcomes, by forcing life to match my vision instead of allowing it to unfold.

And the only way through that wall was to stop pushing against it.

The only way forward was to let go.

This book is an invitation to explore what happens when you finally release your grip. When you stop trying to force the river to flow uphill. When you trust that maybe, just maybe, the universe knows what it's doing even when you don't understand the path.

It's an invitation to discover that the thing you've been so afraid of, letting go, might actually be the key to everything you've been trying so hard to grasp.

Are you ready to find out what happens when you finally stop doing it the hard way?

Are you ready to discover the power of the undo?

Let's begin.

The journey from clutching to allowing, from forcing to flowing, from exhaustion to ease, it starts with a simple recognition: What if everything you've been taught about getting what you want has been backwards?

Welcome to The Undo Principle. Welcome to doing less and receiving more. Welcome to the most counterintuitive, liberating, powerful approach you've ever tried.

Welcome to letting go.

PART ONE: THE TRUTH ABOUT TRYING TOO HARD

Why Your Grip Is Suffocating Your Dreams

The Moment It All Came Crashing Down

The first time I realized I might be the problem, I was standing in the self-help section of a bookstore at eleven o'clock on a Tuesday night.

I'd ducked in after another brutal day at work, the kind where you smile so much your face hurts and agree to things you don't want to do and then drive home wondering who that person was who kept saying "absolutely, happy to help!" when inside you were screaming.

I found myself gravitating to the manifestation books like I always did. Maybe this one would have the answer. Maybe this author knew the real secret. Maybe if I just read one more book, took one more course, learned one more technique, everything would finally click.

My basket was already full. Another journal (this one promised to "align your frequency with abundance"). A book about quantum manifestation. A deck of affirmation cards. Seventy-three dollars' worth of hope that this time would be different.

And then I saw it.

My own face, reflected in the store window, overlaid on a display of books with titles like "You Are Enough" and "Stop Seeking Approval" and "Break Free from People-Pleasing."

I looked exhausted. More than that, I looked haunted. Like someone being chased by something they couldn't name.

The basket dropped from my hands. Cards and journals scattered across the floor. A woman nearby gave me a concerned look, asked if I was okay.

I wasn't. I'd been standing in that bookstore, or ones just like it, twice a month for three years. How many books had I bought? How many courses had I taken? How much money had I spent trying to fix whatever was broken inside me?

And here I was again. Back at square one. Still searching. Still broken. Still not enough.

"Ma'am?" the woman said again.

I left everything on the floor and walked out.

That's when the real breakdown started. Not the crying in the car kind from before, this was different. This was the slow-motion collapse of someone who'd been holding themselves together through sheer willpower and finally ran out of will.

The Unraveling

Over the next two weeks, I started noticing things I'd been too busy "working on myself" to see.

Like how I hadn't talked to my best friend from college in eight months. I'd been too busy with my morning routine, my evening routine, my weekend workshops and webinars and courses. She'd stopped reaching out. I didn't blame her.

Like how I ate the same breakfast every single day, not because I liked it, but because some manifestation guru said it was "high vibration." I didn't even remember what foods I actually enjoyed anymore.

Like how I'd been seeing the same therapist for two years and we spent every session talking about my manifestation goals. Had I ever once talked about how I actually felt? Did I even know how I felt anymore, or had I trained myself to only feel what I was supposed to feel?

Like how I'd stopped listening to music unless it was specifically designed to "raise your frequency." No sad songs allowed. Nothing too heavy. Only positive, uplifting, high-vibe music. When did I become afraid of my own playlist?

Like how I couldn't watch a movie without analyzing whether it aligned with my vision. Couldn't have a conversation without checking if the other person's energy was "right." Couldn't make a decision without consulting my intuition, my tarot cards, my pendulum, and at least three different manifestation experts on YouTube.

I had become so controlled that I'd lost all sense of who I was beneath the control.

The manifestation version of me didn't drink coffee after noon, always got eight hours of sleep, meditated twice daily, and never complained. She was positive, grateful, high-vibe, and constantly working on her personal growth.

But who was I? The real me, underneath all that?

I didn't know anymore. And that terrified me more than anything.

The Breaking Point

It happened at my desk on a random Thursday afternoon.

I was writing in my manifestation journal, something I did every day at 3 PM, right after my "mid-afternoon alignment check." I was supposed to write about how grateful I was for everything coming my way, how excited I was about my expanding reality, how aligned I felt with my highest timeline.

My pen froze over the page.

I couldn't write another word. Not one more lie disguised as manifestation.

Because that's what it had become, hadn't it? Lying. To myself, to the universe, to my journal. Performing gratitude I didn't feel. Faking excitement about a future I wasn't even sure I wanted anymore. Pretending everything was unfolding perfectly when in reality, I felt like I was slowly disappearing.

My hands started shaking. Then my whole body. I closed the journal, shoved it in my desk drawer, and just sat there, staring at my computer screen, feeling something I hadn't let myself feel in years:

Nothing.

Not positive. Not negative. Just... empty.

And the strangest thing happened in that emptiness, I felt the tiniest flicker of something that might have been relief.

What Manifestation Culture Gets Wrong About Control

Here's something I wish someone had told me three years earlier, before I spent all that money and time and energy trying to manifest my way to happiness: manifestation culture is selling you a very specific type of anxiety disorder and calling it empowerment.

I don't say this lightly. I say it as someone who developed actual OCD-like symptoms from manifestation practices. Who couldn't leave the house without checking my vision board. Who had panic attacks if I missed my morning affirmations. Who believed, genuinely believed, that one negative thought could destroy everything I'd built.

Let me break down what modern manifestation culture actually teaches you to do:

You must monitor every single thought. Because your thoughts create your reality, you have to catch the "bad" ones before they manifest into bad experiences. This means being hypervigilant about your own mind 24/7.

Think about what that actually means, you're essentially teaching yourself that your own thoughts are dangerous.

You must perform positivity at all times. Feeling sad? That's a low vibration that will attract more sadness. Feeling angry? You're blocking your blessings. Feeling anxious? Well, now you're anxious about being anxious because anxiety attracts more things to be anxious about. You're not allowed to be human anymore. You have to be a perpetual positivity machine.

You must decode everything as a sign. That bird that flew past your window? Sign. The song that came on the radio? Message from the universe. The fact that you stubbed your toe? Probably means you're out of alignment. You spend so much mental energy trying to interpret reality that you forget to actually live in it.

You must work on yourself constantly. There's always another block to clear, another limiting belief to release, another shadow to integrate. You're never quite there yet. Never quite healed enough, aligned enough, high-vibe enough. The goalpost keeps moving, and you keep chasing.

You must control your words. Because you're "speaking things into existence," you have to police every casual statement. Can't say "I'm so broke" even as a joke. Can't say "this is killing me" about a tough project. Can't even say "I'm dying for a coffee" without worrying you're manifesting death. Language becomes a minefield.

Does any of this sound like freedom to you? Does it sound like empowerment?

Or does it sound like being told your own mind is an enemy you must constantly battle?

The Illusion of Control

The fundamental problem is that manifestation culture has convinced us that we can control things we actually cannot control. And in trying to control the uncontrollable, we make ourselves sick.

You cannot control what thoughts arise in your mind. You can choose what to do with them once they arise, but the initial arising? That's not under your conscious control. Neuroscience has shown this definitively. You become aware of a thought milliseconds after your brain has already generated it.

But manifestation culture tells you that you must control every thought, which means you're trying to do something that's neurologically impossible. And when you inevitably fail, because you will fail, because it's impossible, you blame yourself. You must not be spiritual enough yet. Must need to work harder on your mindset.

You cannot control what emotions you feel. Emotions arise from the limbic system, the ancient part of your brain that's been keeping humans alive for hundreds of thousands of years. When you feel fear, sadness, anger, these are adaptive responses, not personal failures.

But manifestation culture tells you these emotions are dangerous, that they'll lower your vibration and attract negativity. So you try to suppress them, which neuroscience tells us leads to more intense emotions, more anxiety, and a whole host of mental health issues.

You cannot control other people. This seems obvious, but so much manifestation advice is based on trying to manifest other people's behaviors. Manifest your ex back. Manifest your boss giving you a raise. Manifest your mother-in-law respecting your boundaries. You're essentially being taught to try to control other human beings through the power of your thoughts. When it doesn't work, you're told you just need to believe harder.

You cannot control timing. The universe doesn't run on your schedule. Life is complex. There are billions of variables influencing when and how things unfold. But manifestation culture sells you the idea that if you just align properly, you can speed things up. Then when things don't happen when you want them to, you're told you must be blocking it somehow.

Here's what you can control: your actions, your responses, your focus, your values, how you treat people, what you do with your time.

But manifestation culture barely focuses on these things. It's all about trying to control your thoughts, your emotions, other people, timing, all the things you actually can't control.

And that's a recipe for profound helplessness disguised as empowerment.

The Victim-Blaming Disguised as Wisdom

The most insidious part of manifestation culture is how it turns every bad thing that happens to you into your fault.

Got sick? You must have been holding onto toxic emotions.

Lost your job? Your vibration wasn't aligned with abundance.

Got cheated on? You must have subconsciously believed you weren't worthy of loyalty.

Experienced trauma? You attracted it with your frequency.

This isn't spiritual wisdom. This is victim-blaming wrapped in pretty packaging.

I watched a woman in one of my manifestation groups share that she'd been diagnosed with breast cancer. She was terrified, reaching out for support.

You know what the responses were?

"What limiting beliefs do you think created this?"

"Your body is just showing you what needs to be healed emotionally."

"Remember, you're creating your reality. What is this trying to teach you?"

Not one person said, "I'm so sorry. That's terrifying. How can I support you?"

The entire framework had made us incapable of basic human compassion. Everything had to be a lesson, a manifestation, a sign. Nothing could just be the painful randomness of living in a body in a complex world.

This woman was going through one of the hardest things a human can experience, and instead of getting support, she got a metaphysical interrogation about what she'd done wrong to create it.

That's when I started to understand: this isn't about empowerment. This is about control. And not the kind that actually helps you, the kind that just gives you someone to blame when life gets hard. Even if that someone is yourself.

The Science of Why Forcing Fails

After my bookstore breakdown, I became obsessed with understanding why trying harder wasn't working. Not from a spiritual perspective this time, I'd read enough of that. I wanted to understand the actual biology and psychology of what was happening in my body when I was in that state of desperate forcing.

What I found was fascinating. And infuriating. Because it turns out, the harder you try to force something, the more you activate the exact brain states that make it impossible to achieve.

The Nervous System Nobody Talks About

Your autonomic nervous system, the part that operates below conscious awareness, has several distinct states. Dr. Stephen Porges mapped this out in his Polyvagal Theory, and understanding it changed everything for me.

Ventral vagal state: This is your optimal state. You feel safe, connected, open. Your social engagement system is online. You can think creatively, see possibilities, connect with others, and yes, receive good things that come your way. This is the state where manifestation actually happens.

Sympathetic state: This is fight-or-flight. You're mobilized, activated, ready for action. Your heart rate increases. Your muscles tense. Your vision narrows. This state is great if you're running from a bear. It's terrible if you're trying to live your life. In this state, you can achieve things through force, but it's exhausting and unsustainable.

Dorsal vagal state: This is freeze or shutdown. When stress becomes overwhelming, your system collapses into numbness, disconnection, depression. You've given up, not through choice but through nervous system overwhelm.

Here's what nobody in the manifestation world told me: when you're desperately trying to force something to happen, when you're gripping, grasping, affirming from a place of need, you're in sympathetic activation.

Your body is in fight-or-flight mode.

And in fight-or-flight, your nervous system prioritizes immediate survival over everything else. It shuts down or reduces:

- Creative thinking (your prefrontal cortex, the planning center, goes partially offline)
- Ability to see opportunities (you get tunnel vision, literally and figuratively)
- Connection with others (you become guarded and defensive)

- Digestion and immune function (energy diverts to muscles for fighting or fleeing)
- And most critically: **your ability to receive and integrate new things**

Your body cannot receive when it's in survival mode. It can only defend.

Every time you desperately visualize from a place of "I need this or I'm not okay," every time you anxiously check whether your affirmations are working, every time you force yourself to stay positive because you're terrified of attracting negativity, you're telling your nervous system that you're unsafe.

And an unsafe nervous system is a closed system.

What Your Brain Does When You Force

There's a region of your brain called the anterior cingulate cortex. It's involved in monitoring for errors and conflicts. When you're trying to force something, when there's a gap between what is and what you're trying to make happen, this region lights up like a Christmas tree.

It's constantly checking: Are we there yet? Did it work? Why isn't it working? What's wrong?

This creates what neuroscientists call "cognitive load." Your brain is using so much energy monitoring and controlling that it has less available for actually moving toward what you want.

Meanwhile, your prefrontal cortex, the part of your brain responsible for planning, decision-making, and creative problem-solving, starts to go offline. Under chronic stress and constant forcing, you literally become less able to think clearly and see solutions.

So you're working harder but thinking worse. Trying more but achieving less. The forcing itself is making you less effective.

The Reticular Activating System Trap

Your RAS, the Reticular Activating System, is like a filter in your brain. It determines what you notice and what you ignore out of the millions of bits of sensory information coming at you every second.

Manifestation teachers love to talk about this. "Focus on what you want and your RAS will help you see opportunities!" True. But incomplete.

Because your RAS works differently depending on what state your nervous system is in.

When you're relaxed and in ventral vagal (that safe, connected state), your RAS has a wide aperture. It can notice opportunities, synchronicities, possibilities. It highlights things that could help you.

When you're stressed and in sympathetic (fight-or-flight), your RAS narrows dramatically. It focuses almost exclusively on threats, problems, and obstacles. This made sense evolutionarily, when you're running from danger, you need to notice other potential dangers, not opportunities.

So that state of desperate wanting? That anxious "why isn't it here yet?" energy? That's telling your RAS to scan for threats.

You're literally programming your brain to notice everything that's going wrong while being blind to what's going right.

I experienced this directly. When I was in my most desperate manifesting phase, I started keeping a "manifestation evidence journal" to track all the signs that my desires were coming. I'd spend thirty minutes every night trying to find proof that it was working.

And you know what I found? Nothing. Or worse than nothing, I found evidence it wasn't working. Which made me panic and try harder, which made me more stressed, which made my RAS narrow further, which made me see even less evidence.

It was a death spiral, all caused by trying too hard.

Why Affirmations Can Backfire Spectacularly

In 2009, researchers Joanne Wood, John Lee, and Elaine Perunovic published a study in Psychological Science that found positive self-statements can actually make people with low self-esteem feel worse.

They had participants with varying levels of self-esteem repeat statements like "I am a lovable person" while measuring their mood.

People with high self-esteem felt a bit better. People with low self-esteem, the ones who supposedly needed the affirmations most, felt significantly worse.

Why? Because of something called "cognitive dissonance." When what you're saying is too far from what you believe, your brain experiences that gap as threatening. It highlights all the evidence that contradicts what you're affirming.

So when you're broke and you affirm "I am financially abundant," your brain immediately brings up: the overdue bills, the empty bank account, the fact that you can't afford groceries. The affirmation doesn't override these thoughts, it amplifies them.

This creates more stress, which triggers more sympathetic nervous system activation, which makes you even less able to receive or create what you want.

The affirmations that work are the ones that create a believable bridge from where you are to where you want to be. Not giant leaps your nervous system rejects, but small steps it can accept.

But manifestation culture doesn't teach you that. It teaches you to affirm the end result as if it's already true, which for most people just creates internal conflict and more stress.

The Dopamine Depletion Cycle

Here's something else I learned: when you're constantly in forcing mode, you're depleting your dopamine.

Dopamine is often called the "reward" neurotransmitter, but it's more accurate to call it the "wanting" neurotransmitter. It's what drives motivation and desire.

When you're constantly chasing, constantly trying to force outcomes, constantly focused on what you don't have yet, you're activating your dopamine system over and over without the actual reward.

It's like revving your car engine while the car is in park. You're burning fuel but going nowhere.

Over time, this depletes your dopamine reserves. You become less motivated, less energized, more prone to depression and anhedonia (inability to feel pleasure).

I lived this. The more I forced, the more depleted I became. The more depleted I became, the harder I had to try to feel anything. The harder I tried, the more depleted I became.

It was a vicious cycle that no amount of manifestation techniques could fix. Because the techniques themselves were causing the problem.

The Beautiful Prison You're Building

Three years into my manifestation journey, my life looked impressive from the outside. I had a morning routine that would make any productivity guru weep with joy. I had systems and trackers for everything. My apartment was organized according to feng shui principles. I ate a perfect diet, exercised religiously, meditated daily, journaled constantly.

I was the picture of someone who had their shit together.

I was also completely miserable.

Because I'd built what I now call the beautiful prison, a life that looks successful, organized, and intentional from the outside but feels suffocating from the inside.

How the Prison Gets Built

The beautiful prison doesn't appear overnight. It's constructed gradually, one well-intentioned rule at a time.

It starts innocently enough. You read a manifestation book that says visualization is key. Okay, you'll visualize every morning. Just fifteen minutes.

That works for a while. You feel empowered. In control. Like you're finally doing something productive with your life.

Then you read another book that says you also need to affirm throughout the day. So you set reminders on your phone. Every hour, stop and affirm.

Still manageable. You're being proactive. Taking charge of your reality.

Then someone tells you about the importance of gratitude journaling. Add that to the evening routine. Thirty minutes before bed, write down everything you're grateful for. Focus on what you want to attract more of.

Your routine is getting longer, but that's fine. This is important work. Self-development requires dedication.

Then you learn about the power of visualization boards. Spend a weekend creating the perfect board. Make sure to look at it every single day. Feel the feelings.

And the importance of meditation for raising your vibration. Add that. Twenty minutes in the morning, twenty at night.

And tracking angel numbers and synchronicities. Better start a journal for that too.

And monitoring your thoughts. Can't let negative ones slip through. Better check in every thirty minutes to make sure you're thinking right.

And being careful about your words. Speaking things into existence means every casual phrase matters.

And curating your environment. Only high-vibe music. Only inspirational content. Only positive people.

And checking your alignment. Are you in the right energy? Better do a quick meditation to check.

Before you know it, you're spending three to four hours a day on manifestation practices. Your entire life has become organized around trying to manifest a better life. You have no time to actually live because you're too busy trying to create the perfect conditions for living.

The Rules That Become Bars

I didn't realize I was in a prison until I tried to take a day off.

It was a Saturday. I woke up exhausted. My body was screaming for rest. I thought: maybe I'll just skip my routine today. Sleep in. Do nothing.

The panic was immediate and overwhelming.

What if skipping one day ruins everything? What if my vibration drops and I attract something terrible? What if this is the universe testing my commitment?

I got up and did my full routine. All three hours of it. With resentment building in my chest the entire time.

That's when I started seeing the bars.

The bar of consistency: I must do my practices every single day or everything will fall apart.

The bar of positivity: I must maintain a high vibration at all times. Negative emotions are dangerous.

The bar of vigilance: I must monitor my thoughts, my words, my energy constantly. One slip could ruin everything.

The bar of perfection: I must do the practices correctly. If they're not working, it's because I'm not doing them right.

The bar of isolation: I must distance myself from anything or anyone that might lower my vibration.

The bar of worthiness: I must keep working on myself because I'm clearly not there yet.

Each rule I thought was empowering me was actually imprisoning me.

What It Actually Costs You

The beautiful prison extracts a price. Several prices, actually.

You lose spontaneity. Everything must be planned, analyzed, checked for alignment. When was the last time you did something on a whim? Followed an impulse? Said yes to something without first checking your intuition and your calendar and your energy levels?

You lose authentic relationships. You can't be around "low-vibe" people, even if they're going through something hard. You can't be vulnerable because vulnerability might attract more reasons to be vulnerable. You perform positivity instead of showing up as you actually are.

You lose rest. Real rest. The kind where you're not doing anything productive or working toward becoming better. You've turned rest into another form of work, meditation isn't rest if you're using it to try to manifest something.

You lose presence. You're so busy monitoring whether you're in the right state to receive that you're never actually here. You're analyzing your experience instead of having it.

You lose yourself. The real you, underneath all the manifestation practices and routines and rules. You've optimized yourself right out of existence.

I realized this one morning when someone asked me what I wanted for breakfast.

I froze. I didn't know. I'd been eating the same "high-vibration" breakfast for so long that I'd completely forgotten what I actually enjoyed eating.

Such a small thing. But it cracked something open in me.

How many other parts of myself had I lost? How much of my life was built around rules instead of genuine desire?

The Keeper of Your Own Cage

Here's the most painful realization: I was both the prisoner and the guard.

Nobody was forcing me to do these practices. Nobody was punishing me when I skipped them, except me. I'd internalized every rule so deeply that I'd become my own jailer.

The voice in my head that said "you're not doing enough" wasn't my mother or my boss or some manifestation guru. It was me.

The anxiety about missing a day? Mine. The guilt about having negative thoughts? Mine. The fear that everything would fall apart if I stopped trying so hard? All mine.

I'd built this prison brick by brick, rule by rule, and I was the one keeping myself locked inside.

Which meant, and this is where it gets interesting, I was also the only one who could set myself free.

But first, I had to admit something I'd been avoiding for three years:

It wasn't working.

Not really. Not in the ways that mattered.

I'd manifested some things, sure. But I'd also manifested anxiety, exhaustion, disconnection, and a constant sense that I was never quite good enough.

The beautiful prison was still a prison.

And I was so, so tired of being my own warden.

REFLECTION QUESTIONS

Before moving to the next chapter, sit with these questions. Don't rush to answer them. Let them percolate.

What rules govern your daily life that you didn't consciously choose?
Write them down. See them on paper. Notice which ones actually serve you and which ones are just bars you've built.

When was the last time you did something purely for joy, without checking if it aligned with your goals?
If you can't remember, what does that tell you?

What are you afraid will happen if you stop trying so hard?
Be specific. What's the fear underneath the effort?

If you weren't allowed to work on yourself for an entire month, who would you be?

Strip away all the practices, the routines, the constant self-improvement. What's left?

Don't answer these in the way you think you should. Answer them honestly. The beautiful prison was built on shoulds.

Freedom starts with truth.

PART TWO: THE RELEASE REVELATION

Understanding the Power of Letting Go

The Paradox: Wanting Without Needing

My grandmother used to grow the most spectacular tomatoes. Deep red, perfectly ripe, bursting with flavor. People would stop by just to see her garden, to ask for her secrets.

I remember asking her once, when I was maybe ten years old, "Abuela, how do you make them grow so big?"

She laughed. "Mija, I don't make them do anything. I give them what they need, good soil, water, sunshine. And then I let them be. The growing happens on its own."

"But don't you worry about them?" I asked. Even then, I was a worrier.

"Why would I worry? Worrying doesn't make them grow faster. It just makes me tired." She plucked a tomato from the vine and handed it to me. "The secret is knowing when to tend and when to trust."

I didn't understand what she meant. Not then. Not until I was sitting in that parking lot at 2 AM, twenty years later, having a breakdown because I'd been trying to force my entire life to grow according to my timeline, my blueprint, my desperate need for control.

That conversation came back to me. The tomatoes. The tending and trusting. The way she could want a bountiful harvest without clutching the plants so tightly that she choked the life out of them.

This is the paradox at the heart of everything: you have to want it without needing it.

The Difference That Makes All the Difference

There's a moment in every relationship where you can feel the shift from wanting to needing. You go from "I enjoy being with this person" to "I can't live without this person." From "This relationship adds to my life" to "This relationship is the only thing keeping me alive."

And the instant you cross that line, the instant wanting becomes needing, something fundamental changes in the energy between you.

The person can feel it. They can sense the desperation, even if you never say it out loud. Your texts become slightly too eager. Your availability becomes slightly too constant. Your happiness becomes slightly too dependent on their mood, their attention, their approval.

You think you're showing them how much you care. What they're actually experiencing is the weight of being responsible for your emotional survival.

And what happens? They pull away. Not because they're cruel or playing games, but because needing is heavy. It's suffocating. It turns love into obligation and joy into pressure.

This same dynamic plays out with everything you're trying to manifest.

When you want something, you're in a state of desire. You can see it, imagine it, move toward it. But you're also still okay without it. You're complete as you are, and this thing would be an addition, an enhancement, a delicious expansion of what's already good.

When you need something, you're in a state of desperation. You've decided that your okayness depends on having it. That you're broken, incomplete, insufficient until it arrives. Every moment without it is evidence that something is wrong with you, wrong with the universe, wrong with reality itself.

Wanting says: "This would be wonderful."
Needing says: "I will die without this."

Wanting is open-handed.
Needing is white-knuckled.

Wanting can receive.
Needing can only grasp.

My Coffee Shop Revelation

I figured this out in the strangest place: a coffee shop line.

I'd been trying to manifest a new job for six months. Not just any job, the perfect job. I had a list of seventeen specific requirements. I visualized daily. I affirmed constantly. I checked job boards obsessively, applied to anything that was even close, interviewed with a desperation I tried to hide but definitely didn't.

Nothing was working. In fact, the more I tried, the worse the interviews went. I'd walk in already needing them to hire me so badly that I couldn't just have a conversation. I was performing, proving, desperately trying to be whoever they wanted me to be.

That day, I'd had another rejection email. Another "we've decided to go in a different direction." I was in line for coffee, trying not to cry, when I overheard the conversation in front of me.

Two women, clearly friends catching up. One was saying, "So I wasn't even looking for a new job, you know? I loved where I was. But this opportunity just fell in my lap, and it was too good to pass up."

Something in me snapped.

Of course. Of course she got the perfect opportunity when she wasn't even looking. Of course it came to her easily when she didn't need it. When she was already content. When she was open-handed instead of white-knuckled.

I thought about my grandmother's tomatoes. She wasn't standing over them, desperately needing them to grow. She wanted a good harvest, sure. But she was also fine if some didn't make it. She'd still eat. She'd still be okay.

That's when it hit me: my desperation was the block.

Not my limiting beliefs. Not my worthiness issues. Not my misaligned chakras or my low vibration or any of the other things I'd been obsessively working to fix.

Just the simple fact that I needed a new job so badly that I couldn't receive one.

The Physics of Desire vs. Desperation

Think about magnetism for a second. Two magnets will attract each other when they're aligned correctly. But if you try to force two magnets together in the wrong orientation, they repel. The harder you push, the more they push back.

Desire is like magnets in correct alignment. There's a natural pull. Things flow.

Desperation is like magnets in repelling orientation. You're pushing so hard that you're actually creating resistance. The more force you apply, the more you push away what you want.

I saw this play out over and over once I started noticing it.

My friend Rachel had been trying to get pregnant for three years. Fertility treatments, supplements, tracking every single cycle, timing everything perfectly. The more she needed it, the more elusive it became. Finally, she and her husband decided to take a break, maybe look into adoption. Within two months of truly letting go of the need, not giving up on wanting a child, but releasing the desperate grip on how and when it had to happen, she got pregnant naturally.

My colleague Marcus had been chasing a promotion for years. Staying late, volunteering for everything, making it crystal clear that he wanted to move up. He was passed over repeatedly. Then he got a job offer from another company, a good one, one he was genuinely considering. Suddenly he didn't need his current company to promote him anymore. He had options. He had power. Within a week, his boss offered him the promotion he'd been chasing. The instant he didn't need it, it appeared.

My cousin had been desperately trying to find love. Dating apps, matchmakers, saying yes to every setup. The harder she looked, the worse the dates got. Then she decided to take a year off from dating entirely, to focus on herself and her life. She joined a hiking group, not to meet people but because she'd always wanted to explore more trails. She met her now-husband on the third hike. When she wasn't looking. When she didn't need it.

This pattern is everywhere once you see it. And it's not some mystical universal law, it's basic psychology and biology.

What Happens in Your Body

When you need something desperately, your body interprets that need as danger.

"I need this or I won't survive" is a survival message. Your autonomic nervous system hears that and says, "Got it, we're in emergency mode."

Your sympathetic nervous system activates. Stress hormones flood your system. Your body prepares to fight or flee. Your pupils dilate, your muscles tense, your heart rate increases, your digestion slows.

In this state, your prefrontal cortex, the part of your brain responsible for creativity, problem-solving, and long-term planning, starts to go offline. Blood flow redirects to the parts of your brain that handle immediate threats.

You become narrowed. Focused on the threat (the lack of what you need). Unable to see possibilities or opportunities. Defensive rather than open.

And remember what we learned in the last chapter: in this state, you literally cannot receive. Your nervous system is closed, defended, in survival mode.

But when you want something without needing it, when you can hold desire without desperation, your body stays in what's called ventral vagal activation. You're in rest-and-digest mode. Safe, open, connected.

In this state, your prefrontal cortex stays online. You can think creatively. You can see opportunities. You're open to connection and receptivity.

This is the state where synchronicities happen. Where opportunities arise. Where you're in the right place at the right time and you actually notice.

Not because the universe is rewarding you for having the right vibration. But because your nervous system is in the state that allows you to perceive and receive what's available.

How to Want Without Needing

This is where it gets practical. Because "just stop needing it" isn't helpful advice. If you could simply decide not to need something, you would have already done it.

The shift happens through a different door: making yourself okay without it.

Not pretending you're okay. Not spiritual bypassing or toxic positivity. Actually cultivating genuine okayness in your life as it is right now.

When I was desperate for that job, my whole sense of self was tied up in getting it. I'd told myself that once I got the right job, then I'd be successful. Then I'd be worthy. Then I'd be enough.

As long as I believed that, I would always need it. Because without it, I was nothing.

The shift came when I started asking myself: What if I'm already enough? What if I'm already worthy, right now, in this job I don't even like? What if my value isn't contingent on my job title or my salary or impressing anyone?

At first, these felt like empty questions. But I kept asking them. And slowly, something shifted.

I started noticing things I'd been too desperate to see. I was good at my current job, even if it wasn't my dream job. I had colleagues who respected me. I was learning things. I was paying my bills. I was actually, if I was honest, fine.

Not thriving. Not where I wanted to be ultimately. But fine. Okay. Sufficient.

The moment I truly felt that, not thought it, but felt it in my body, everything changed.

I stopped applying to jobs frantically. I stopped checking LinkedIn every hour. I stopped rehearsing interview answers in my head at 3 AM. I started actually living my life, even though it wasn't perfect yet.

And within three weeks, a former colleague reached out about an opportunity. One that wasn't even posted publicly. One that fit me so perfectly it was almost eerie.

I got the job. Not through forcing, but through being open to receiving it when it came.

What Happens When You Finally Unclench Your Fists

Try something with me right now.

Make a tight fist. Clench it as hard as you can. Imagine you're holding something precious and if you relax your grip even slightly, you'll lose it forever. Hold that tension. Notice what it feels like in your hand, your arm, your shoulder. Notice your breathing. Notice your jaw.

Now hold that fist for the next five minutes while you keep reading.

Can't do it, can you? Either you're in pain already, or you've unconsciously relaxed your grip because maintaining that level of tension is unsustainable.

This is what you've been doing with your manifestations. With your goals. With your entire life.

You've been holding on so tight for so long that you've forgotten what it feels like to relax.

My First Release

The first time I consciously practiced letting go, really letting go, not just saying the words, was with my vision board.

I'd had this thing on my wall for three years. I looked at it every single morning and every single night. I'd touch different images and visualize myself into those scenarios. I knew every detail by heart.

And I was so tired of it. So tired of looking at this collage of other people's stock photo lives and trying to convince myself that this was what I wanted. So tired of checking it daily like some kind of manifestation scorecard, tallying what I'd achieved and what I was still failing to bring into reality.

One Saturday morning, I walked over to it, pulled it off the wall, and put it in a drawer.

Just like that. No ceremony. No burning ritual or releasing prayer. I just took it down.

The relief was immediate and overwhelming. Like I'd been holding my breath for three years and finally exhaled.

But relief quickly gave way to terror. What had I just done? Wasn't the vision board essential? Wasn't I supposed to look at it daily to stay aligned with my desires? What if removing it meant I was giving up on my dreams?

I spent that entire day in a low-grade panic, convinced I'd just sabotaged my entire future.

But by the evening, something else started to emerge. A strange sense of spaciousness. Of possibility.

Without the vision board dictating what I was supposed to want, I could ask myself: What do I actually want?

Not what looks good on a vision board. Not what successful people are supposed to want. Not what would prove to my family or my friends or Instagram that I'm doing life right.

What do I, in this moment, genuinely desire?

The answer surprised me. I wanted to take a ceramics class. That's what came up first. Not a bigger goal. Not a promotion or a relationship or a move to a new city. I wanted to play with clay.

It felt almost embarrassingly small. But it was real. It was mine. It was something I wanted without needing it to mean anything about my worth or my success.

So I signed up. Tuesday evenings, a ceramics studio downtown.

The Ripple Effect

That ceramics class changed my life, though not in any way I could have planned.

The teacher was this woman in her sixties named Diane who'd spent thirty years as a corporate lawyer before quitting to open the studio. She didn't know about my manifestation journey or my breakdown or any of it. She just taught me how to center clay on a wheel.

"You can't force it," she said the first night, watching me wrestle with a lump of clay that kept flying off the wheel. "The harder you push, the more it resists. You have to be firm but gentle. Apply pressure, but also let it move. Find the center by feeling, not by forcing."

I started crying right there, hands covered in wet clay, in front of twelve strangers.

Because she wasn't just talking about pottery.

Over the next few weeks, I learned more about letting go from that clay than I had from three years of manifestation courses.

Clay teaches you immediately when you're forcing. It collapses, flies off the wheel, refuses to take shape. There's no faking it. No positive thinking your way through. Either you're working with it or you're fighting it, and the clay makes the distinction very clear.

I learned that you can have a vision for what you want to create, a bowl, a vase, whatever, but the clay has a say too. Sometimes it wants to be taller, shorter, wider than you planned. You can force your vision or you can collaborate. The best pieces come from collaboration.

I learned that mistakes aren't failures. That collapsed pot isn't wasted clay. You wedge it back together and start again. Nothing is ruined beyond repair.

I learned that you can't rush the process. The clay needs to dry at its own pace. The firing happens on its own timeline. You can't make it go faster by wanting it more.

But mostly, I learned what it felt like to do something purely for the joy of doing it. Not to get somewhere. Not to become someone. Not to prove anything. Just to put my hands in clay and see what wanted to emerge.

The Things That Showed Up

Once I started unclenching my fists in one area, it became easier to do it in others.

I stopped checking my bank account five times a day. Not because I suddenly had more money, but because the checking was a form of gripping. I knew how much I had. Checking constantly wasn't helping; it was just keeping me in a state of anxiety about it.

I deleted three manifestation apps from my phone. The ones that sent me reminders to affirm, to visualize, to check my alignment. Every ping was a little jolt of "you're not doing enough." I didn't need that anymore.

I stopped forcing myself to meditate every single day. Some days I did, because I wanted to. Some days I didn't, because I didn't want to. And nothing fell apart.

I started saying no to things. To social obligations that felt like shoulds. To opportunities that looked good on paper but didn't feel right in my body. To courses and workshops that promised to finally fix whatever was still broken in me.

And the weirdest thing happened: my life got better.

Not in dramatic, vision-board ways. In small, real ways.

I started sleeping better, because I wasn't lying awake reviewing whether I'd done enough that day to deserve my manifestations.

My friendships deepened, because I stopped curating them based on whether people were "high-vibe" and started just being honest about where I was.

Money started flowing more easily, not because I'd manifested it, but because I wasn't operating from panic anymore. I could think clearly about opportunities. I could negotiate from a place of worth instead of desperation.

And yes, things I'd been trying to force for years started showing up. But not because I'd finally figured out the right technique or cleared the right block.

They showed up because I'd finally gotten out of my own way.

The Difference Between Giving Up and Letting Go

My mother called me about two months into my "letting go" experiment.

"Sofia, are you okay?" she asked, concern thick in her voice. "Your sister said you took down your vision board. And you quit that online course you were taking. Are you... giving up?"

I understood why she was worried. From the outside, it probably looked like I was having some kind of breakdown. Going from super-motivated manifestation devotee to someone who'd removed all her manifestation tools in a matter of weeks.

"I'm not giving up," I told her. "I'm letting go. There's a difference."

"Isn't that the same thing?" she asked.

It's not. But I understand why it looks that way. From certain angles, letting go and giving up can look identical. The person who's given up and the person who's let go both might have stopped chasing, stopped forcing, stopped trying so hard.

But the internal experience is completely different. And the outcomes are completely different.

What Giving Up Actually Is

Giving up is collapse. It's what happens when you've been trying so hard for so long that you just can't anymore. Your system is exhausted. Your hope is depleted. You're done, not through wisdom but through burnout.

Giving up feels like: "I can't do this anymore. It's too hard. I'm too tired. Nothing I do works anyway. What's the point?"

Giving up is passive. It's surrender in the worst sense, not surrender to something greater, but surrender to defeat.

When you give up, you stop taking any action at all. You collapse into hopelessness. You tell yourself that you were stupid for wanting it in the first place, that it was never meant for you, that you should just accept your lot and stop reaching for more.

Giving up leaves you feeling flat, depressed, resigned. There's no peace in it. Just numbness and disappointment.

I've given up before. I know what it feels like. After my last relationship ended, the one before my awakening, I gave up on love for a while. I deleted all the dating apps, but not from a place of trusting my own timeline. From a place of "I'm unlovable and all men are terrible and I'm just going to get seventeen cats and be done with it."

That's giving up. And it didn't feel good. It felt like defeat.

What Letting Go Actually Is

Letting go is release. It's an active choice to stop gripping, stop forcing, stop trying to control something that doesn't want to be controlled.

Letting go feels like: "I still want this. I'm still moving toward it. But I don't need to death-grip it anymore. I can hold it lightly. I can trust."

Letting go is active. It's surrender in the best sense, not to defeat, but to a wisdom larger than your individual will. To flow instead of force. To timing you can't see yet but are willing to trust.

When you let go, you don't stop taking action. You stop taking desperate action. You don't stop wanting. You stop needing. You don't stop having vision. You stop strangling the vision with your grip.

Letting go leaves you feeling spacious, peaceful, open. There's relief in it. Freedom. A sense of "whatever happens, I'm going to be okay."

The ceramics class was letting go. I still wanted to create things. I still wanted to express myself. I just stopped forcing it to happen through manifestation techniques and instead let it happen through playing with clay.

The job situation was letting go. I still wanted a better job. I still applied to opportunities that felt right. I just stopped applying to everything frantically and let the right thing find me.

The vision board was letting go. I still had dreams and desires. I just stopped trying to control exactly what they looked like and when they arrived.

The Test That Tells You Which One You're Doing

Here's how you can tell the difference: What happens when you think about your desire?

If you've given up, thinking about it brings a wave of defeat. Heaviness. Resignation. "Yeah, that thing I wanted that will never happen."

If you've let go, thinking about it brings a wave of lightness. Openness. Curiosity. "Yeah, that thing I want. I wonder how it'll unfold."

Giving up closes you. Letting go opens you.

Giving up says, "It's impossible." Letting go says, "It's possible, just not on my rigid timeline or in my prescribed way."

Giving up feels like an ending. Letting go feels like a beginning.

Your Nervous System Is Listening

Here's something I wish I'd understood years earlier: your nervous system is like a highly sensitive antenna. It's picking up on everything, not just the words you say or the thoughts you think, but the state you're in.

And it's responding accordingly.

When your nervous system feels safe, it opens you up to connection, creativity, and receiving. When it feels unsafe, it closes you down to defend and protect.

Every manifestation technique you've been taught tries to work at the level of thoughts or words or actions. But that's not where the real power is. The real power is at the level of your nervous system.

Because your nervous system doesn't care what you visualize if you're visualizing from a state of panic. It doesn't care what you affirm if you're affirming from a state of desperation. It doesn't care what you write in your journal if your body is in fight-or-flight while you write it.

The state matters more than the content.

The Body Knows

I learned this in the most visceral way during a particularly intense manifestation meditation.

I was following a guided visualization about calling in abundance. The instructor had us imagine money flowing to us from all directions, see our bank accounts growing, feel the feelings of financial freedom.

I was doing everything "right." Eyes closed, breathing deeply, really trying to feel it.

But my body was tense. My jaw was clenched. My shoulders were up by my ears. My stomach was in knots.

And suddenly I realized: I was trying to feel abundant while my body was in a state of threat. I was trying to visualize receiving while my nervous system was locked in defense mode.

No wonder it wasn't working.

The visualization was saying "abundance and safety." My body was screaming "danger and scarcity."

And the body always wins.

You can't think your way into a new nervous system state. You can't visualize or affirm your way out of sympathetic activation. Your body needs actual evidence of safety, not imaginary evidence.

What Actually Regulates Your Nervous System

After I figured this out, I went deep into learning about nervous system regulation. Not from manifestation teachers, but from trauma therapists, somatic practitioners, neuroscientists.

What I learned changed everything.

Your nervous system regulates through:

Physical safety. Do you have food, shelter, physical security? If your basic needs are genuinely threatened, no amount of positive thinking will convince your body it's safe.

Connection. Are you in relationship with people who see you, accept you, make you feel like you belong? Isolation is a nervous system stressor. Connection is regulating.

Movement. Physical movement, especially rhythmic movement, helps discharge stress and return your system to regulation. This is why walking, dancing, or swimming often help more than sitting meditation when you're activated.

Breath. But not the way you think. Not forcing deep breaths when you're activated, that can actually make it worse. Gentle lengthening of your exhale signals safety to your vagus nerve.

Present-moment sensation. Actual sensory input grounds you. The feeling of your feet on the floor. The temperature of air on your skin. The taste of food. This brings you out of your anxious mind and into your sensing body.

Play and joy. Real play, not productivity disguised as fun, is deeply regulating. It tells your nervous system that you're safe enough to engage in non-essential activities.

Letting go of what you can't control. This is the big one. When you stop trying to force outcomes, you stop sending your nervous system constant danger signals. Release is inherently regulating.

None of these are what manifestation culture teaches. Manifestation culture is often actively dysregulating, it keeps you in a state of "not enough yet," which is a threat state.

The Practice That Changed Everything

I started doing something radical: before any manifestation practice, I would regulate my nervous system first.

Not through visualization or affirmation. Through simple somatic practices.

I'd put my feet flat on the floor and feel the ground beneath them. I'd place my hand on my heart and feel it beating. I'd look around the room and name things I could see: blue mug, green plant, wooden table.

I'd ask my body: What do you need right now to feel safe?

Sometimes the answer was movement. I'd do jumping jacks or shake my body. Sometimes it was stillness. I'd just sit and breathe. Sometimes it was connection. I'd text a friend or call my grandmother.

Only after I felt genuinely settled, not forced calm, but actual regulation, would I think about my desires or goals.

And the shift was profound.

When I visualized from a regulated state, it felt completely different. Not like forcing or performing or trying to convince myself. More like... remembering something that already existed. Touching into a possibility that felt real and available.

When I affirmed from a regulated state, the words didn't feel like lies. They felt like truths I was growing into.

When I took action from a regulated state, the actions felt inspired instead of desperate. I wasn't chasing; I was responding to what was right in front of me.

The outcomes changed too. Not because I'd finally mastered the technique, but because I'd finally changed the state I was operating from.

Your Body Is Manifesting

Here's the truth they don't tell you: your body is manifesting all the time. Not through your thoughts or your vision boards or your affirmations.

Through your nervous system state.

When you're in fight-or-flight, you manifest more things to fight or flee from. Not because of some mystical law of attraction, but because your RAS is scanning for threats and your behavior becomes defensive and contracted.

When you're in freeze/shutdown, you manifest stagnation. Not because you're not aligned, but because your system is too depleted to move toward anything.

When you're in ventral vagal, that safe, open, connected state, you manifest connection, opportunities, synchronicities. Not because you're finally vibrating correctly, but because you're finally open to receiving what's available.

The manifestation happens through your state, not through your strategies.

And the fastest way to shift your state isn't through more techniques or practices or trying.

It's through letting go.

Because letting go is the ultimate regulation. It's telling your nervous system: we don't have to control this. We can trust. We're safe enough to be open.

And an open nervous system can receive what a defended one never could.

PRACTICE: THE UNCLENCH

Before moving to the next chapter, try this:

Physical unclenching. Make tight fists. Hold them for thirty seconds. Notice the tension. Now release. Let your hands open completely. Notice the relief. This is what letting go feels like in your body.

Mental unclenching. Think of something you're trying to force. Something you need desperately. Ask yourself: "What if I want this but don't need it? What if I'm okay either way?" Notice what happens in your body when you ask this.

One small release. Choose one manifestation practice you do out of obligation or fear, not joy. Just for one week, don't do it. Notice what happens. Does everything fall apart? Or do you just breathe a little easier?

This isn't giving up. This is practicing the difference between gripping and allowing.

Your nervous system will thank you.

PART THREE: THE IDENTITY TRAP

Who You Are vs. Who You're Becoming

The Old You Is Fighting for Its Life

I was sitting across from my therapist, Christine, six months after my parking lot breakdown, and she said something that stopped me cold.

"Sofia, has it occurred to you that maybe you're not stuck because you don't know how to move forward? Maybe you're stuck because some part of you is terrified of who you'll become if you do."

I stared at her. "That doesn't make any sense. Why would I be afraid of becoming the person I'm working so hard to be?"

She leaned forward. "Because becoming someone new means the current you has to die. And no organism goes willingly toward its own death, even when that death is necessary for growth."

I wanted to argue with her. I wanted to say she was wrong, that I wasn't afraid of change, I was desperate for it. I'd been trying to change for years. Every morning routine, every vision board, every affirmation was about becoming someone different, better, more.

But later that night, lying in bed, her words kept circling back.

Some part of you is terrified.

I thought about the times I'd self-sabotaged just when things were going well. The job interview I'd shown up late to after having the perfect outfit laid out the night before. The date with someone I actually liked where I'd picked a fight over nothing. The writing project I'd been excited about until I sat down to start it, then suddenly had seventeen urgent errands to run.

I'd always called these moments "resistance" or "blocks" or "limiting beliefs." Things to overcome, to push through, to clear.

But what if they were something else? What if they were the current version of me fighting to stay alive?

The Identity I Didn't Know I Had

Here's something nobody tells you about personal growth: your identity is a biological imperative, not just a psychological construct.

Your brain has spent your entire life gathering evidence about who you are. Every experience, every interaction, every success and failure has been catalogued and compiled into a story: This is who I am. This is what I'm capable of. This is where I fit in the world.

That story becomes your identity. And your brain treats that identity like a matter of survival.

Because in our evolutionary past, knowing who you were in your tribe, your role, your value, your place, was literally a matter of life and death. If you lost your identity, you lost your belonging. And losing your belonging meant exile, which meant death.

Your brain still operates on that ancient programming. Even though being "the anxious one" or "the people-pleaser" or "the one who never follows through" isn't actually keeping you safe, your brain thinks it is.

Because it's familiar. It's known. It's been working well enough to keep you alive this long.

So when you try to change, when you try to become someone who's confident instead of anxious, boundaried instead of people-pleasing, consistent instead of scattered, your brain sounds the alarm.

Danger. Unknown territory. Threat to survival.

And it deploys every tool in its considerable arsenal to get you back to the familiar, safe identity it knows.

I saw this play out with brutal clarity after I quit my toxic job.

I'd been "the over-achiever who stays in terrible situations way too long" for my entire adult life. It was my pattern. High school boyfriend who treated me badly? Stayed for two years. College major that crushed my soul? Stuck it out for four years and graduated with honors. First job out of college with a boss who yelled daily? Three years before I left.

I thought my identity was "dedicated" or "loyal" or "someone who doesn't give up easily."

What I actually was, was someone whose sense of self depended on enduring suffering to prove my worth.

So when I quit that job, when I finally chose myself over proving something, I had a full-blown identity crisis.

Without suffering to endure, who was I?

Without a toxic situation to stay loyal to, what was my value?

Without sacrificing myself, did I even exist?

The Morning I Didn't Recognize Myself

About three weeks after quitting, I woke up and didn't know who I was.

Not in a poetic, existential way. In a genuine, disorienting way.

I'd always been someone with a morning routine. Up at 5:30 AM, no matter what. Workout, shower, perfect outfit, out the door looking like I had everything together even when I was falling apart inside.

But that morning, I had nowhere to be. No job to prove myself at. No schedule to keep. No performance to maintain.

I could sleep until nine if I wanted. I could stay in pajamas all day. I could do absolutely nothing and no one would know or care.

The freedom I'd been craving felt like free-falling.

I got up and stood in front of my closet. All those carefully curated outfits, the power suits, the statement necklaces, the shoes that said "successful professional woman." Who was I dressing for anymore?

I found myself reaching for the same black blazer I'd worn to every important meeting for the past two years. My hand was actually on it when I realized: I was trying to put on my old identity like a costume. Because without it, I didn't know who I was.

I sat down on the floor of my closet and cried.

Not sad crying. Scared crying. The kind that comes from feeling unmoored, undefined, like if you don't know who you are then maybe you don't exist at all.

My grandmother found me there an hour later. She'd let herself in with the key I'd given her, calling out my name, getting worried when I didn't answer.

"Mija, what happened?"

"I don't know who I am anymore," I said, and it came out as a wail.

She sat down next to me, right there on the closet floor, her old knees creaking. "Good," she said.

I stared at her. "Good?"

"Yes, good. You're not supposed to know who you are right now. You're in between. The old you is dying and the new you hasn't been born yet. This is the hardest part. But

it's also the most important part. This is wh
change happens."

"It feels terrible," I said.

"Of course it does. Death always feels terrible. Even when it's necessary."

What You Have to Die to in Order to Be Reborn

My friend Maya is a therapist who works primarily with people going through major life transitions. Over coffee one day, about a month into my identity crisis, I asked her what she tells clients who are stuck between who they were and who they're becoming.

"I tell them the truth," she said. "Which is that transformation is a death and rebirth process. And most people try to do the rebirth part without doing the death part. They want to become someone new while still being who they've always been. And that's impossible."

"So what has to die?" I asked.

She pulled out a napkin and drew a diagram. At the top, she wrote "OLD IDENTITY." At the bottom, "NEW IDENTITY." And in the middle, a long list.

"Everything in the middle has to die," she said.

This is what she wrote:

The Stories That Define You

"I'm not good at math."
"I'm an anxious person."

"I'm not the type who takes risks."
"I always choose the wrong partners."
"I'm bad with money."
"I'm too sensitive."
"I'm not creative."

These stories feel like facts. They feel like descriptions of reality. But they're not. They're narratives you've created from cherry-picked evidence, and they've become self-fulfilling prophecies.

To become someone new, you have to let these stories die. Even the ones that feel true. Especially the ones that feel true.

I realized I'd been telling myself "I'm someone who needs to work harder than everyone else to be worthy" since I was seven years old, when my second-grade teacher told my parents I was "trying very hard" in a tone that suggested trying hard was what you did when you weren't naturally smart.

That story shaped everything. Every all-nighter in college. Every weekend spent working when friends were out having fun. Every relationship where I worked harder at loving them than they worked at loving me.

The story had to die for me to become someone who believed their existence was valuable without the suffering.

The Relationships That Confirm Who You Think You Are

This one hurt the most.

Some relationships in your life exist to keep you exactly as you are. Not because the people are bad or malicious, but because they know you in a certain way, and that's the version of you they're comfortable with.

When you start to change, these relationships become uncomfortable for both of you.

I had a friend, let's call her Jessica, who I'd known since college. Our entire friendship was built on commiserating. We'd meet for wine and spend three hours complaining about our jobs, our love lives, our families. We bonded over our shared victimhood, our mutual overwhelm, our matching anxiety.

It was comfortable. It was safe. It confirmed for both of us that this was just how life was.

When I started my letting-go journey, when I started choosing differently, when I stopped being available for the three-hour complaint sessions, Jessica got weird.

"You've changed," she said one night, and it wasn't a compliment.

"I hope so," I said. "I've been trying to."

"You're different. You're not as fun anymore. You're too... I don't know. Too positive or something. It's like you think you're better than everyone now."

I wasn't trying to be better than anyone. I was just trying to be different than I'd been. But to Jessica, my transformation was a threat. Because if I could change, what did that say about her staying the same?

We don't talk much anymore. And I had to grieve that. Even though the relationship wasn't healthy, it was familiar. It was part of my identity: "I'm someone who has a best friend who gets me."

Letting it die felt like cutting off a limb.

The Behaviors That Prove You're You

Your identity isn't just stories and relationships. It's patterns of behavior that feel like "just who I am."

For me, it was overcommitting. I was the person who said yes to everything. Who volunteered before being asked. Who stayed late, took on extra projects, helped everyone with everything.

I thought this made me valuable. Helpful. Good.

What it actually made me was exhausted and resentful. But it was my identity. "I'm someone people can count on." "I'm the reliable one." "I'm the helper."

To become someone different, I had to let that die. I had to start saying no. I had to let other people figure out their own problems. I had to disappoint people.

And every time I did, every cell in my body screamed that I was doing it wrong. That I was being selfish. That I was going to lose everyone.

My identity was fighting for its life.

The Environments That Keep You Comfortable

Physical spaces hold energy. Not in a woo-woo way, in a very real, neurological way. Your brain associates certain environments with certain versions of yourself.

My apartment was set up for the old me. The vision boards on every wall. The manifestation altar in the corner. The bookshelf full of self-help books. The motivational quotes taped to my bathroom mirror.

Every surface was covered in reminders of who I was supposed to be trying to become.

After my breakthrough, I looked around one day and realized: this isn't a home. It's a constant self-improvement seminar.

I spent a weekend taking it all down. The vision boards went into storage. The altar got dismantled. The motivational quotes came off the mirrors. I donated half my self-help books.

My apartment looked naked afterward. Empty. But also... peaceful.

For the first time in years, I could just exist in my space without being reminded of all the ways I wasn't enough yet.

The environment that had supported my old identity had to die too.

The Version of Success You've Been Chasing

This was the hardest death of all.

I'd spent my entire adult life chasing a very specific definition of success: corner office, six-figure salary, impressive title, perfect relationship, beautifully curated life that looked good on Instagram.

None of these were actually my dreams. They were borrowed dreams. Cultural programming. Things I thought I was supposed to want.

But they'd become my identity. "I'm someone who's ambitious. Who wants more. Who's going places."

To become who I actually wanted to be, someone creative, someone free, someone who valued depth over achievement, I had to let that version of success die.

And with it, I had to let die the approval of everyone who measured me by that old definition.

My mother's pride in being able to tell her friends what I did for a living.
My college friends' envy of my career trajectory.
My own sense that I was winning at life.

All of it had to die.

The Cost of Your Current Identity

Here's the question no one wants to ask: What is your current identity costing you?

Not in some abstract, spiritual way. In concrete, specific ways. What are you not doing, not having, not becoming because of who you think you are?

I made a list. A brutally honest one. Here's what my identity as "the over-achieving, manifestation-obsessed, always-trying-to-improve person" was costing me:

Sleep. Years of it. Because I couldn't rest if I hadn't done enough that day to earn it.

Spontaneity. I couldn't do anything on a whim. Everything had to be checked against my goals, my vision, my alignment.

Deep relationships. I'd curated my entire social circle based on whether people were "on the same path" rather than whether I actually enjoyed being around them.

Creative expression. I'd turned everything into a productivity project. Even hobbies had to have a purpose, a goal, an outcome.

Presence. I was never actually here. Always thinking three steps ahead, planning, strategizing, optimizing.

Joy. Just simple, uncomplicated joy. I didn't remember what it felt like to enjoy something without analyzing it or trying to make it mean something about my growth.

My body. I'd treated it like a vehicle to get me to my goals, not like a home to live in. I ate "high-vibe" foods I didn't like. I worked out in ways that felt like punishment. I ignored signals of exhaustion because rest was for people who weren't dedicated enough.

My actual desires. Underneath all the borrowed dreams and manifested goals, what did I actually want? I had no idea. That voice had been silenced for so long I couldn't hear it anymore.

When I saw it all written out, when I really let myself feel the cost, something cracked open in me.

I'd been so busy trying to become someone impressive that I'd completely abandoned someone real: me.

The Identity Tax

Every identity you hold has a maintenance cost. Like a subscription you're paying for without realizing it.

If your identity is "I'm not good with money," the tax is staying bad with money. Because if you suddenly got good with money, you'd have to update your story about yourself. And that's harder than just staying financially chaotic.

If your identity is "I'm the responsible one who always has it together," the tax is never being able to fall apart. Never being able to ask for help. Never being able to be human and messy and imperfect.

If your identity is "I'm someone who's been through trauma and that's why I can't do hard things," the tax is staying stuck in that narrative even when you've done years of healing and are actually capable of more than you think.

I had a client once, I started coaching people through the release process after my own transformation, who was stuck in the identity of "I'm not someone who finishes things."

She had seventeen unfinished projects. Books she'd started writing but abandoned. Courses she'd enrolled in but never completed. Relationships she'd let fade. Jobs she'd left before seeing them through.

Every abandoned project reinforced her identity: "See? I told you. I'm not a finisher."

But here's what we discovered: finishing things would have meant updating her entire self-concept. It would have meant letting go of the story her mother had told her when she was eight: "You're so smart, but you never stick with anything. You're just not that type of person."

She'd carried that story for thirty years. It had become her identity. And finishing something, anything, would mean that story was wrong. Would mean her mother was wrong. Would mean she'd wasted decades believing a lie.

The identity tax was high: seventeen abandoned dreams. But the cost of letting the identity die felt even higher: admitting her mother's story wasn't true meant reconstructing her entire sense of self.

Eventually, she chose to pay the higher price. She finished one project, a children's book she'd been working on for five years. It wasn't perfect. It wasn't publishable. But it was done.

The day she wrote "The End," she called me sobbing. "I don't know who I am anymore."

"Good," I told her, echoing my grandmother. "Now you get to find out."

How to Hold Your Vision Without Strangling Your Evolution

Six months into my identity transformation, I went back to ceramics class.

I'd stopped going for a few weeks during the worst of the identity crisis. Too overwhelmed to do anything but survive the death of who I'd been.

But I missed it. I missed the clay, the wheel, the simple pleasure of making things.

Diane, my teacher, noticed immediately that something was different about me.

"You're looser," she said, watching me center a new piece. "Your hands are softer. What changed?"

"I stopped trying so hard to be someone," I said.

She smiled. "I can tell. Look what you're making."

I looked down. For weeks, I'd been trying to make perfect, symmetrical bowls. They'd all collapsed or come out wobbly. But this thing on my wheel wasn't a bowl at all. It was organic, asymmetrical, completely unplanned. And it was beautiful.

"I wasn't trying to make this," I said.

"I know," Diane said. "That's why it's working. You stopped forcing it to be something specific and let it become what it wanted to be."

I stared at the clay, and suddenly understood something fundamental about transformation.

The Paradox of Becoming

You can have a vision for who you want to become. But you can't force yourself into that vision. You can't manufacture it through sheer will.

Because who you're becoming isn't something you create. It's something you discover.

It's already there, underneath all the layers of who you think you're supposed to be. Under the programming and the stories and the borrowed identities.

Your job isn't to build someone new from scratch. It's to remove everything that's covering up who you already are.

Like Michelangelo said about sculpting David: "I saw the angel in the marble and carved until I set him free."

You're not creating yourself. You're revealing yourself.

But here's the catch: you can't reveal yourself while clutching the old identity. You have to let go of who you think you are in order to discover who you actually are.

The Practice of Identity Flexibility

After my grandmother's closet-floor wisdom, I started working with what I call "identity flexibility", the ability to hold your sense of self lightly instead of rigidly.

Here's what that looked like practically:

I stopped using permanent language about myself. Instead of "I am anxious," I started saying "I'm experiencing anxiety right now." Instead of "I'm not creative," I'd say "I haven't developed my creativity yet."

Small shifts, but they opened up possibility. Because if I am something permanently, I can't change it. But if I'm experiencing something temporarily, it can shift.

I started trying on different versions of myself like clothes. What would the spontaneous version of me do today? What would the boundaried version of me say here? What would the rested version of me choose?

I wasn't being fake. I was experimenting. Exploring different ways of being to see what felt authentic.

I got curious about who I was when no one was watching. What did I do when I didn't have to perform being anyone? What did I reach for when I wasn't trying to impress or improve or become?

The ceramics class was part of this. Nobody there knew about my manifestation journey or my career or anything. I could just be someone who played with clay. And in that space, I found parts of myself I'd forgotten existed.

I gave myself permission to contradict my own story. Just because I'd always been one way didn't mean I had to stay that way. Just because everyone knew me as the over-achiever didn't mean I couldn't become the person who knew when to rest.

Every contradiction was a small death of the old identity and a small birth of something new.

Holding the Vision Lightly

I still have dreams. I still have desires. I still have a vision for my life.

But I hold it differently now.

Before, my vision was rigid. A detailed blueprint that life had to follow exactly or I'd failed. The manifestation practice was all about forcing reality to match my blueprint.

Now, my vision is more like a direction. A north star. I know where I want to go, but I'm flexible about the route. I'm open to detours, to unexpected paths, to discovering that maybe the destination I thought I wanted isn't actually where I need to be.

Before, my vision required me to be a specific person, confident, successful, perfectly aligned, always high-vibe.

Now, my vision allows me to be whoever I'm becoming. Messy, uncertain, in-process. The vision doesn't require me to be someone I'm not. It invites me to discover who I am.

Before, the gap between who I was and who I wanted to be felt like failure.

Now, the gap feels like possibility. Like space to grow into. Like room to breathe.

The vision hasn't changed that much, honestly. I still want similar things, meaningful work, authentic relationships, creative expression, freedom, peace.

What's changed is my grip on how that has to look and who I have to be to deserve it.

I'm not strangling the vision anymore. I'm moving toward it gently. Curiously. With trust that who I need to become to receive it is already emerging, already being revealed, already here underneath the layers I'm learning to shed.

REFLECTION: WHO WOULD YOU BE?

Before moving to the next chapter, try this thought experiment:

If you woke up tomorrow with total amnesia, no memory of your past, no knowledge of who you've been, no stories about who you are, who would you be?

Without the story that you're not creative, what would you make?
Without the story that you're not good with people, who would you connect with?
Without the story that you always fail at X, what would you attempt?
Without the story that you're just not that kind of person, what kind of person would you be?

This isn't about erasing yourself. It's about seeing how much of who you think you are is just story. And stories can be rewritten.

What would you do if your current identity wasn't at stake?

If you could try something without it meaning anything about who you are or aren't, what would you try?

These questions aren't meant to be answered quickly or easily. Sit with them. Let them work on you. Let the old identity squirm a little at the possibility of dying.

Because on the other side of that death, you're waiting.

The real you. The one who was always there, underneath everything you thought you had to be.

And that version of you? They don't need to be manifested or created or improved into existence.

They just need to be freed.

PART FOUR: LETTING GO OF OUTCOMES

Releasing Your Attachment to How It Has to Happen

Why You Need to Stop Micromanaging the Universe

The first time I tried to bake bread from scratch, I failed spectacularly.

I'd found this elaborate recipe online, artisanal sourdough, the kind that takes three days and seventeen steps and makes you feel like a domestic goddess when you post photos of it on Instagram. I followed every instruction to the letter. I measured everything precisely. I set timers. I checked the temperature constantly. I hovered over the dough like a nervous parent.

The result? A dense, inedible brick that could have been used as a doorstop.

My grandmother, who'd been baking bread for sixty years, watched my obsessive process with amusement. "Mija, you're trying too hard. Bread needs attention, yes, but it also needs space. You keep opening the oven to check it, you're letting out all the heat. You keep poking it to see if it's ready, you're deflating it. The bread knows how to become bread. Your job is to create the conditions, then get out of the way."

"But what if it doesn't turn out right?" I asked.

She shrugged. "Then you eat mediocre bread. But at least you ate bread instead of exhausting yourself trying to control every molecule of the dough."

I didn't understand what she meant. Not then.

But two years later, when I was trying to control every aspect of my manifestation journey with the same micromanaging energy I'd brought to that bread recipe, her words came back to me.

You're trying too hard. Create the conditions, then get out of the way.

The Illusion of Control

Here's what I finally understood: I wasn't trying to manifest things. I was trying to control reality itself.

I had detailed plans for exactly how everything needed to unfold. Not just what I wanted, but when, how, who should be involved, what it should look like, what it should feel like, which exact route it should take to get to me.

My vision board wasn't a vision board, it was a military operation plan.

I knew exactly what month I'd get the promotion. I knew exactly what my future partner would look like, sound like, believe in. I knew exactly what neighborhood I'd live in and what my apartment would look like down to the color of the throw pillows.

And I genuinely believed that this level of specificity was what made manifestation work. That the universe needed precise GPS coordinates to deliver my desires.

What I was actually doing was boxing in possibility until there was only one acceptable outcome. One narrow path. One specific way things could be "right."

Everything else? Failure.

This is what micromanaging the universe looks like:

You don't just want a relationship, you want a relationship that starts exactly like it did in your visualization. You meet at a coffee shop. He orders his drink right after you. Your eyes meet. You both reach for the cinnamon at the same time and laugh. Anything else, meeting on an app, being set up by friends, reconnecting with someone from your past, doesn't count. It's not the "right" way.

You don't just want financial abundance, you want it from a specific source in a specific amount by a specific date. A $10,000 raise by March 1st from your current company. When you get a $12,000 freelance opportunity in February, you're disappointed. It's not what you planned.

You don't just want to feel better, you want to feel better through a specific healing modality using specific techniques in a specific timeframe. When you start feeling better through something you didn't expect, you distrust it. It wasn't on your healing plan.

This isn't manifestation. This is trying to write the universe's to-do list.

When I Tried to Control My Way to Love

After my toxic relationship ended, I did what any good manifestation student would do: I made a list.

Not just any list. The list. Thirty-seven specific qualities my future partner had to have.

Emotionally available. Financially stable. Loves to travel but also appreciates staying home. Morning person. Health-conscious but not obsessive. Good with kids. Close with his family but not enmeshed. Reads books. Likes hiking. Has a dog but not a cat because I'm allergic. Votes the same way I do. Shares my spiritual beliefs. Makes me laugh. Challenges me intellectually. Is taller than me but not too tall. Has green or blue eyes. Works in a creative field but has stable income.

And on and on.

I took this list to my manifestation coach, who praised it. "Excellent! The more specific, the better. The universe loves clarity!"

So I visualized this person every day. I could see his face, well, a composite face I'd created from various stock photos. I could hear his laugh. I could feel his hand in mine.

I went on dates and measured every person against the list. Most failed immediately. Too short. Wrong eye color.

Doesn't hike. Wrong job. Cat owner. Deal breaker after deal breaker.

The few who made it past date one still fell short. Maybe they had 28 of the 37 qualities, but those missing nine? Unacceptable. This wasn't my person. The universe was still searching for my exact specifications.

Then I met James.

He wasn't on the list. Not even close.

He was a night owl, not a morning person. He'd never left the country. He didn't have any pets because he traveled for work. He was shorter than my "requirement." He had brown eyes. He worked in finance, which I'd literally written "NO" next to on my list because I'd dated a finance guy who'd broken my heart.

On paper, he was all wrong.

In person, he was... right. In a way I couldn't explain or plan or control.

He made me laugh until I couldn't breathe. He listened like listening was an art form. He challenged me in ways that made me grow but never made me feel small. He was kind to waiters and remembered details about my stories and cried during movies and cooked elaborate dinners on Sunday nights.

But I almost didn't give him a chance. Because he wasn't what I'd ordered from the universe.

I remember calling my friend Rachel after our third date, confused. "He's not the person I manifested. He's not on my list."

"Do you like him?" she asked.

"Yes, but, "

"Sofia. Do you like him?"

"...Yes."

"Then maybe your list was wrong. Maybe you don't actually know what's best for you."

That should have been a revelation. Instead, it made me angry. Of course I knew what was best for me! I'd spent months visualizing it! I'd written thirty-seven specific requirements! I'd been so clear about what I wanted!

Except what I'd actually been was controlling. Demanding. Trying to reduce the infinite complexity of human connection to a checklist the universe had to follow.

I went on one more date with James, then broke it off. He wasn't the plan.

Six months later, I was still single, still miserable, still measuring every person against my impossible list.

And James? He was engaged to someone else. Someone who didn't need him to be a character in her pre-written story.

The Plans You Make vs. The Life You're Meant to Live

My friend Alex is a yoga teacher. About eight years ago, she had her entire life planned out with military precision.

She was going to build her yoga business to 100 students within two years. She was going to open her own studio by year three. She was going to develop a signature method and trademark it. She was going to write a book. She was going to become one of those Instagram-famous yoga teachers with 100K followers. She was going to do teacher trainings around the world.

She had vision boards. Business plans. Content calendars mapped out for six months at a time. A detailed five-year plan with quarterly benchmarks.

"I know exactly where I'm going," she told me over coffee, spreading out her plans across the table with pride. "I'm not leaving this to chance."

Then her mother got sick. Stage four cancer, sudden and devastating.

All those plans? They evaporated instantly.

Alex moved back home. She taught private yoga sessions to pay bills, but mostly she was a caregiver. She held her mother's hand through chemo. She learned about hospice care. She sat with her mother through the final weeks, the final days, the final hours.

Her mother died eight months after the diagnosis.

According to her five-year plan, Alex should have been running her studio by then. Instead, she was planning a funeral and sorting through her mother's belongings and trying to figure out who she was in a world without the person who'd raised her.

"I felt like such a failure," she told me a year later. "Everything I'd planned for, everything I was working toward, none of it happened. I'd spent so much energy trying to control my future, and then life just... happened. And my plan was completely irrelevant."

"But then something shifted?" I asked, because I could see it in her face, something had changed.

She nodded. "During Mom's last week, she was in and out of consciousness. But there was this one afternoon when she was really present, really here. And she looked at me and said, 'Alex, you make beautiful plans. But don't miss the life that's happening while you're busy planning the life you think you're supposed to have.'"

Alex paused, tears forming. "That night, she asked me to teach her some gentle stretches. Nothing major, just movements to help her feel less stiff, less disconnected from her body. So I did. Right there in her hospice bed, I guided her through the gentlest yoga sequence I've ever taught.

"And she smiled. Really smiled, for the first time in weeks. She said, 'This is what yoga is for. This moment. This connection. This is the whole point.'"

Alex's voice cracked. "She died two days later. And I realized, all my plans about growing my business, getting famous, building some kind of yoga empire... I'd completely lost sight of why I loved yoga in the first place.

It wasn't about the metrics or the followers or the studio. It was about moments exactly like that one with my mom. Presence. Connection. Being of service in the most ordinary, profound ways."

She never opened that studio. Never wrote that book. Never became Instagram-famous.

Instead, she started working with people going through loss and transition. She teaches yoga in hospices and grief centers. She sits with people in their darkest moments and helps them find their breath.

"It's nothing like I planned," she said. "And it's everything I was meant to do. But I had to let go of every single plan to find it."

When the Plan Becomes the Prison

There's a saying I love: "We plan, God laughs."

Not because there's some cosmic force mocking our attempts to direct our lives, but because our plans are built from such limited information.

You're planning from where you are right now. From what you know right now. From who you are right now.

But you're going to grow. Things are going to happen. Information is going to reveal itself. Opportunities you can't even imagine yet are going to emerge.

And if you're rigidly attached to your plan, you'll miss all of it.

I see this all the time with people who've been manifesting for years and feel stuck. When I ask them about their vision, they pull out these elaborate plans they created three, four, five years ago. And they're still trying to force those exact outcomes, even though they themselves are completely different people now.

"Do you even want that anymore?" I ask.

They pause. "I mean... I've been working toward it for so long. I can't just give up now."

But it's not about giving up. It's about recognizing that you made that plan with limited information, limited perspective, and a limited version of yourself.

Holding onto it isn't dedication. It's refusing to grow.

The plan was meant to serve you, not imprison you.

The Difference Between Vision and Rigidity

I want to be clear: I'm not saying you shouldn't have vision. I'm not saying you shouldn't set goals or make plans.

I'm saying there's a difference between vision and rigidity.

Vision says: I want to feel fulfilled in my work. I want to use my gifts to serve others. I want to make a good living doing something meaningful.

Rigidity says: I will be the VP of Marketing at a tech company by age 35, making exactly $150,000, working remotely Tuesday through Thursday, with a team of six people, in the SaaS industry specifically.

Vision says: I want a loving, committed partnership where I feel seen, appreciated, and challenged to grow.

Rigidity says: I will meet my future husband at a friend's wedding in September, he will be 6'1" with green eyes, work in architecture, and propose after exactly 18 months of dating on a beach in Mexico.

See the difference?

Vision is directional. It points you toward what matters. But it leaves room for life to surprise you. Room for better possibilities than you could imagine. Room for paths you didn't know existed.

Rigidity is prescriptive. It demands that life follow your script exactly. And when it doesn't, which it won't, you either miss what's actually available or exhaust yourself trying to force reality to comply.

How to Trust Without a Map

The scariest question I ever asked myself was: "What if I can't see the whole path from here?"

I was sitting in my ceramics class, working on a piece that kept collapsing. Every time I tried to make it into the bowl I'd envisioned, it fell apart. Finally, in frustration, I stopped trying to control what it was becoming and just responded to what the clay was doing.

It became something I never planned. Organic. Asymmetrical. Completely different from my original vision.

And it was the best thing I'd made.

Diane, my teacher, came over. "That's beautiful. What is it?"

"I have no idea," I said honestly. "It wasn't what I was trying to make."

"The best pieces never are," she said. "You planned for a bowl. The clay wanted to be a sculpture. You could have fought it and ended up with a mediocre bowl, or you could work with it and end up with something you couldn't have imagined."

She paused, then added, "That's how most things in life work, you know. You can have a plan. But you also have to trust the material you're working with, including yourself, including circumstances, including the mystery of it all. Trust without a map."

"But how do you know where you're going if you don't have a map?" I asked.

"You don't. That's the whole point. That's where faith lives, in the not-knowing."

What Faith Actually Means

I'd been using the word "faith" wrong for years.

I thought faith meant believing so strongly in my vision that it had to come true. Faith as in certainty. Faith as in knowing the outcome so clearly that doubt was impossible.

That's not faith. That's denial.

Real faith is trusting that you'll be okay even when you don't know how things will turn out.

Faith is not: "I know this will work out exactly as I've planned."
Faith is: "I don't know how this will work out, but I trust I can handle whatever comes."

Faith is not: "The universe will give me exactly what I asked for."
Faith is: "Whatever I receive, even if it's different from what I requested, is probably what I actually need."

Faith is not: "If I just believe hard enough, I can control the outcome."
Faith is: "I can let go of control and trust the unfolding."

This kind of faith is terrifying. Because it requires acknowledging how little control you actually have. How much you don't know. How many variables are completely outside your influence.

But it's also liberating. Because it means you can stop exhausting yourself trying to control the uncontrollable.

My Map-less Journey

I started practicing this accidentally.

After my breakdown, after letting go of my vision boards and my detailed plans, I found myself in this strange in-between space. I had some sense of direction, I knew I wanted work that felt meaningful, relationships that felt real, a life that felt like mine.

But I had no idea how to get there. No roadmap. No clear next steps.

The old me would have panicked. Would have made seventeen new plans to fill the void. Would have found a new guru or system or method to follow.

The new me just... sat with it. The not-knowing. The uncertainty.

At first, it was excruciating. My brain kept demanding: What's the plan? What are we doing? Where are we going?

I didn't have answers. So I started asking different questions.

Not "What should I do?" but "What feels alive right now?"

Not "Where am I going?" but "Where am I being pulled?"

Not "What's the right next step?" but "What's the next true step?"

The ceramics class was a next true step. It had nothing to do with my career or my life plan. It was just something that felt alive when nothing else did.

That class led to meeting Diane, whose wisdom about clay became wisdom about life. Which led to conversations about her journey leaving law. Which led to her introducing me to someone who ran a grief center, just as a "you two should meet."

That meeting led to me volunteering one afternoon a week. Which led to discovering I had a gift for holding space for people in transition. Which led to training in grief counseling. Which led to the work I do now, which is nothing like anything I'd ever planned but is exactly what I was made for.

None of this was on my vision board. None of it was in my five-year plan. I couldn't have planned it because I didn't know it existed.

But each small step, taken without knowing where it led, built a path I could never have mapped.

The Practice of the Next True Thing

When people ask me now how to move forward without a plan, I teach them what I call "the next true thing."

You don't need to see the whole path. You just need to see the next step. And not even the "right" step, just the true step.

The step that feels aligned with who you're becoming, even if you can't explain why.

The step that feels alive, even if it doesn't make strategic sense.

The step that calls to you, even if it doesn't fit your plan.

For me, that first true step was ceramics. It made no logical sense. It didn't advance my career or help me manifest my goals or check any boxes. But it felt true.

What's your next true thing? Not the thing you think you should do. Not the thing that would look good on Instagram or impress your family or prove you're not giving up.

What's the thing that, when you imagine doing it, makes you feel just slightly more alive?

It might be small. It might seem unrelated to your big goals. It might make no sense to anyone else.

Do it anyway.

Then, from that place, ask again: What's the next true thing?

Step by step, not knowing where you're going, you'll end up exactly where you need to be.

What Opens Up When You Stop Forcing the Path

My grandmother had this story she loved to tell about a river.

There was a river that decided it wanted to reach the ocean. It could see the ocean in the distance, this vast blue promise. And it wanted to get there as fast as possible.

So instead of following its natural path, meandering through valleys, around mountains, gathering streams, it tried to go in a straight line. It tried to cut through the mountain directly.

The mountain didn't budge. The river exhausted itself trying to force through solid rock. It became frustrated, bitter. "Why won't this mountain move? Why is the universe blocking me from my destiny?"

Meanwhile, another river took the long way around. It wandered. It curved. It took what looked like detours. It didn't fight the landscape; it worked with it. Found the path of least resistance. Gathered tributary streams along the way, becoming bigger and stronger.

Both rivers eventually reached the ocean. But the first one arrived depleted, diminished, angry. The second arrived full, powerful, having nourished everything along its path.

"The ocean doesn't care how you get there," my grandmother would say. "But the journey shapes who you are when you arrive."

I thought about this story constantly as I learned to stop forcing my path.

What I Missed While I Was Forcing

When I look back at those years I spent trying to control every outcome, I can see so clearly now what I was too rigid to notice then:

The opportunities I dismissed because they didn't fit my plan. The job that wasn't quite the title I wanted, but would have led to work I'd have loved. The person who asked me out but wasn't my "type" according to my list. The city I wrote off because it wasn't on my vision board.

The synchronicities I ignored because they weren't the "right" signs. I was so busy looking for specific confirmation that my plan was working that I missed all the universe's gentle course corrections. The repeated book recommendations I brushed off. The recurring conversations about a topic I kept dismissing. The physical symptoms my body was using to tell me something needed to change.

The wisdom in what seemed like obstacles. Every time something didn't work out according to my plan, I interpreted it as a block to clear, a limiting belief to fix, a sign I needed to try harder. I never once considered that maybe it wasn't working out because it wasn't supposed to. That the obstacle was actually protection.

The present moment. I was so focused on the future I was trying to force into existence that I completely missed the life that was happening right in front of me. The conversations I was half-present for because I was visualizing. The sunsets I didn't see because I was journaling. The moments of joy I couldn't fully experience because I was checking whether they aligned with my vision.

The person I actually was becoming. I was so attached to who I thought I needed to be that I didn't notice who I was actually becoming. Someone more patient through the setbacks. More resilient through the "failures." More compassionate through the struggles. The journey was transforming me, but I couldn't see it because I was only focused on the destination.

What Became Possible

The moment I stopped forcing, really stopped, not just said the words, everything shifted.

Not in the ways I expected. Not in the timeline I wanted. But in ways that were so much better than what I'd planned.

Serendipity became possible. When you're following a rigid plan, there's no room for happy accidents. But when you're open, when you're allowing, synchronicities start appearing everywhere. The conversation that leads to an opportunity. The book that falls off the shelf at exactly the right moment. The "chance" meeting that changes everything.

Better outcomes became possible. Remember James, the guy I rejected because he wasn't on my list? I learned later he'd met someone who was perfect for him, someone I never would have found on all my dating apps because she wasn't looking online. Life had better plans for both of us, but I had to let go of my plan to see them.

Growth became possible. When you're forcing a specific outcome, you can't grow beyond the person who made that plan. But when you let go, when you allow yourself to be changed by the journey, you become someone capable of receiving things the old you couldn't even imagine wanting.

Magic became possible. I don't mean woo-woo magic. I mean the real magic of life: the unexpected beauty, the unplanned joy, the gifts you couldn't have asked for because you didn't know they existed. That only shows up when your hands are open enough to receive it.

Rest became possible. This might be the biggest one. When you stop trying to force every outcome, you can finally rest. You don't have to be vigilant every moment. You don't have to control every variable. You can exhale. You can trust. You can let life carry you for a while.

There's a practice I do now when I catch myself trying to force an outcome.

I close my eyes and imagine I'm holding whatever I want in my clenched fists. I feel the tension in my hands, my arms, my whole body from gripping so tight.

Then I imagine slowly opening my hands. Turning my palms up. Still holding the desire, but lightly. Openly. Creating space for it to land if it's meant to, or for something better to arrive instead.

Sometimes my hands want to close again. The instinct to grip is strong. So I just notice that, breathe, and gently open them again.

This isn't giving up. This is allowing.

Allowing means: I want this, but I don't need it to look exactly like my plan.

Allowing means: I'm moving toward this, but I'm open to better routes than the one I've mapped.

Allowing means: I trust that if this specific thing doesn't work out, it's because something more aligned is coming.

Allowing means: I can hold my vision without strangling it.

This is the practice. Not once, but constantly. Every time you notice yourself gripping, forcing, demanding reality comply with your plan:

Breathe. Open your hands. Allow.

PRACTICE: THE OPEN-HANDED EXERCISE

Try this right now:

Physical: Make tight fists. Hold something you want to manifest with white-knuckled intensity. Notice how it feels. The strain. The effort. Now slowly open your hands. Turn your palms up. Hold the same desire, but lightly. Notice the difference in your body.

Mental: Think of something you're trying to force right now. Write down your exact, specific plan for how it has to happen. Every detail. Every timeline. Every specification.

Now write this at the bottom: "Or something better."

That's it. "Or something better." Give the universe permission to surprise you. Give life permission to exceed your limited imagination.

Practical: This week, do one thing with absolutely no outcome in mind. Not because it will lead somewhere or help you manifest something or advance your goals. Just because it feels true. The next true thing. Even if it makes no sense.

Notice what happens when you stop forcing the path and start following the pull.

You might be surprised where it leads. Or more likely, you'll be surprised by how good it feels to finally stop fighting the river and let it carry you home.

PART FIVE: TIME, WORTHINESS, AND TRUST

The Foundation of Receiving

The Illusion That You Can Speed Things Up

I once killed a garden trying to make it grow faster.

Not on purpose, obviously. But I'd planted tomatoes in my first apartment's tiny balcony garden, and I was impatient. I'd read that tomatoes take sixty to eighty days from transplant to harvest, and that felt like an eternity.

So I did everything the internet told me would speed things up. Special fertilizer that promised "rapid growth." Extra watering. Placing aluminum foil around the base to reflect more light. Pruning aggressively. I even played classical music because I'd read that plants respond to vibrations.

I checked those plants constantly. Measured them daily. Googled "why aren't my tomatoes growing faster" at 11 PM. Compared them obsessively to photos online of what they "should" look like at each stage.

The plants got stressed. Overwatered and over-fertilized, they developed yellow leaves and blossom end rot. Most of the tomatoes that did form were small, bitter, and split before they ripened.

My neighbor, Mrs. Chen, grew tomatoes on her balcony too. She planted hers the same week I did. She watered when the soil was dry, gave them sunlight, and otherwise left them alone. She didn't check them daily or measure their progress. She just trusted they were doing what tomatoes do.

Her harvest was abundant. Sweet, perfect tomatoes all summer long.

When I asked her secret, she laughed. "No secret. Just patience. You can't rush a tomato. It needs the time it needs."

"But what if I need tomatoes sooner?" I asked.

She gave me this look, not unkind, but penetrating. "Then you should have planted earlier. Or bought tomatoes from the store. But once you plant a seed, it's out of your hands. The seed has its own timeline. Your job is to support it, not speed it up."

At the time, I thought she was just talking about gardening.

Five years later, having spent countless hours trying to force my manifestations to arrive on my timeline, I finally understood. She was talking about everything.

The Timeline Obsession

There's a special kind of torture in spiritual circles: the question "When will it happen?"

When will I meet my soulmate? When will I get the job? When will my business take off? When will I finally be happy?

And the manifestation industrial complex has made a fortune selling you the illusion that you can control the answer. That if you just use the right technique, hold the right vibration, clear the right blocks, you can speed things up. Manifest in 30 days. Accelerate your timeline. Quantum leap to your desires.

I bought into this completely. I took courses on "rapid manifestation" and "timeline jumping." I learned techniques to "collapse time" between desire and fulfillment. I was convinced that my ability to speed things up was a measure of my spiritual advancement.

Looking back, I can see it clearly: this was just another form of control. Another way my anxiety disguised itself as ambition.

Because here's the truth nobody wants to hear: you can't speed things up.

Not really. Not in any way that matters.

You can work harder, sure. You can take more action. But there are rhythms to life that don't care about your urgency. Seeds need time to germinate. Relationships need time to develop. Healing needs time to integrate. Skills need time to develop.

Some things simply cannot be rushed.

And trying to rush them doesn't make them arrive faster, it just makes you suffer more in the waiting.

What Impatience Actually Costs

I spent three years in a constant state of "not yet."

Not yet successful enough. Not yet healed enough. Not yet manifested enough. Not yet there.

Every moment was just a stepping stone to the next moment, which would be better, which would be closer to my goals, which would finally be enough.

I was always leaning forward into the future, never actually here.

The irony is that all this rushing made everything take longer.

When I was desperately trying to manifest a new job, I went on interviews with such anxious energy that I bombed them. When I finally got a job, I'd already burned myself out so thoroughly that I had no energy left to actually do it well.

When I was rushing to heal my anxiety through aggressive self-improvement, I actually made the anxiety worse. Because rushing is itself an anxiety response. I was trying to anxiously solve my anxiety.

When I was trying to force manifestations to arrive faster, I was in such a state of "not enough" that I couldn't receive them even when they showed up. They never felt like enough because I was always focused on what wasn't here yet.

The rushing cost me the present moment. Which, when you add them all up, cost me years of my life.

The Microwave Generation Meets Ancient Rhythms

We live in the instant gratification era. Two-day shipping. Streaming on demand. Instant messages. Fast food. Same-day delivery.

We've been conditioned to believe that waiting is a problem to be solved. That faster is always better. That if something takes time, there must be something wrong.

But human development doesn't work on Amazon Prime timelines. Neither does growth, healing, or any kind of real transformation.

You don't get to skip the awkward learning phase of a new skill.
You don't get to fast-forward through the tender vulnerability stage of a new relationship.
You don't get to microwave trauma healing that needs to slowly simmer.
You don't get to speed-run the grief process because it's inconvenient.

There are some things that just take the time they take.

And trying to speed them up is like trying to rush a sunset. You can't make it happen faster. You can only ruin your experience of it by being impatient.

The Worthiness Wound That Keeps You Stuck

About eighteen months into my manifestation journey, I was complaining to my therapist Christine that nothing was working.

"I'm doing everything right," I said, listing my daily practices for the hundredth time. "I visualize. I affirm. I've cleared so many blocks. I'm in alignment. So why isn't it manifesting?"

She was quiet for a long moment. Then: "Sofia, can I ask you something?"

"Of course."

"Do you think you deserve what you're trying to manifest?"

"Yes! Obviously. That's the whole point. I've done all the worthiness work. I know I'm worthy."

"That's not what I asked. I asked if you think you deserve it."

I opened my mouth to say yes again, then stopped. Because somewhere deep in my gut, something was screaming NO.

No, I didn't deserve it. Not really. Not just for existing. I could be worthy in theory, in some abstract spiritual sense. But actually deserving of good things? That required earning them. Proving myself. Working hard enough to justify the receiving.

And I'd never worked hard enough. No amount of work would ever be enough.

The Invisible Ceiling

There's a phenomenon in psychology called the "upper limit problem," coined by Gay Hendricks. It's the idea that we all have an unconscious threshold for how much success, love, or happiness we allow ourselves to have.

When we approach that threshold, we unconsciously self-sabotage to bring ourselves back down to a familiar level.

Not because we're broken or self-destructive. But because somewhere along the way, we developed a belief about what we deserve. And that belief functions like a thermostat, keeping us at a certain temperature no matter how hard we try to heat things up.

I watched this play out with a friend who grew up in poverty. She'd worked incredibly hard, put herself through college, built a successful business. By any objective measure, she'd "made it."

But every time her business income went above a certain threshold, about $8,000 a month, something would happen. A client would cancel. Equipment would break. She'd make a costly mistake. Something would bring her back down to around $6,000 a month.

For three years, this pattern repeated. And she kept blaming external circumstances.

Then she did some deeper work and realized: $8,000 a month was more than her parents had ever made. In her family system, making more than your parents did was seen as betrayal. Thinking you were "better than" where you came from.

Her worthiness ceiling wasn't conscious. It was installed when she was seven years old, overhearing her father say that "people who make a lot of money are greedy and forget where they come from."

She didn't consciously believe this anymore. But her nervous system did. And every time she approached that threshold, her system would panic: Danger. We're becoming someone we said we'd never be. We're betraying our people.

The self-sabotage was actually self-protection. Keeping her safe within the bounds of what she unconsciously believed she deserved.

Where Worthiness Wounds Come From

I used to think my worthiness issues came from one or two big traumatic events. And maybe for some people, they do.

But for most of us, the worthiness wound gets created through a thousand small moments. Paper cuts that, over time, become a scar.

The time you were excited about something and were told you were "too much."
The time you succeeded at something and were praised for how hard you worked, not for your innate gifts, teaching you that only effort has value, not just being.
The time love was withheld until you performed correctly.
The time you were celebrated for sacrificing yourself for others, teaching you that your value comes from service, not existence.

The time you were compared to a sibling or peer and came up short.
The time you needed help and were made to feel like a burden.

None of these moments feels traumatic while it's happening. They just feel like normal life. But each one deposits a small belief: "I'm only valuable when I perform. I'm only lovable when I'm useful. I'm only deserving when I earn it."

By adulthood, these deposits have accumulated into a core belief system that runs constantly in the background: I am not inherently deserving of good things. I have to earn everything.

And no amount of affirmations can override a belief system that was installed over decades.

My Worthiness Archaeology

Christine had me do an exercise she called "worthiness archaeology." Going back through my life and identifying the moments that formed my worthiness ceiling.

I found them everywhere:

Age 6: My father telling me I was smart "for a girl." The subtle message: you're not enough as you are.

Age 9: My ballet teacher saying I'd never be a prima ballerina but I could be a "very good supporting dancer" if I worked really hard. The message: excellence isn't available to you, but you can be adequate through effort.

Age 14: My first boyfriend cheating on me, then telling me I was "too intense" and girls should be more "chill." The message: your fullness is too much. Dim yourself to be loved.

Age 19: My college advisor praising me for working three jobs while maintaining good grades, calling me "such a hard worker." Not smart. Not talented. A hard worker. The message: your value is in your labor.

Age 24: My first serious relationship, where I bent myself into a pretzel trying to be what he wanted, and he still left. The message: even your best isn't good enough.

None of these people were trying to wound me. Most thought they were being helpful, realistic, kind even.

But each moment taught me the same lesson: you are not enough as you are. You must earn the right to take up space, to be loved, to receive good things.

By the time I found manifestation culture, I'd spent decades in this belief system. So of course I approached manifestation as something I had to earn through perfect practice.

Of course I couldn't just receive. I had to prove I deserved it first.

And the sickest part? The manifestation world reinforced this wound. It told me that if I wasn't receiving what I wanted, it was because I hadn't worked hard enough on my blocks, my vibration, my alignment.

More earning. More proving. More sacrifice.

The wound dressed up as spiritual growth.

Deserving vs. Earning: The Shift That Changes Everything

The day this finally clicked for me, I was watching a bird at my window feeder.

I'd put out seeds earlier that week, not for any reason, just because I liked watching birds. This sparrow landed, ate some seeds, and flew away.

It didn't do anything to earn those seeds. It didn't prove it was worthy. It didn't work on its limiting beliefs or raise its vibration. It just saw seeds and ate them because that's what birds do.

And I realized: nature understands deserving in a way we've forgotten.

Trees don't earn sunlight. Rivers don't prove they're worthy of flowing to the ocean. Flowers don't do affirmations before they bloom.

They just receive what's available because they're part of the system. They belong here. Their existence is justification enough.

When did we forget that we're part of nature too?

The Paradigm Shift

Here's the shift that changed everything for me:

Old paradigm: I must earn the right to receive good things through hard work, sacrifice, and perfect spiritual practice.

New paradigm: I deserve good things because I exist. My inherent worth is not up for debate.

This sounds simple. It's not.

Because if you really believe the second one, it dismantles your entire relationship with striving, with proving, with the desperate need to be enough.

It means you stop trying to earn love and start allowing yourself to be loved as you are.

It means you stop trying to prove your worth through achievement and start resting in your inherent value.

It means you stop white-knuckling your way to manifestations and start opening your hands to receive what's already trying to reach you.

But making this shift requires confronting a terrifying question: If I don't have to earn my worth, then who am I?

For people whose identity is built on working harder than everyone else, on sacrificing more, on proving their value through constant achievement, this shift feels like death.

Because it is. It's the death of the worthiness wound's grip on your life.

How I Started Practicing Deserving

I started small. Absurdly small.

I allowed myself to sleep in on a Saturday without earning it through working hard all week.

I bought myself flowers just because I wanted them, not because I'd accomplished something.

I said no to a social obligation without a "good excuse."

I let myself rest when I was tired instead of pushing through.

Each tiny act of receiving without earning felt like rebellion. My nervous system screamed that I was being lazy, selfish, irresponsible.

But slowly, so slowly, something shifted.

I started noticing how much energy I'd been spending on the constant calculation: Have I done enough to deserve rest? Have I been good enough to deserve kindness? Have I worked hard enough to deserve success?

The math never added up. There was never enough in the "earned" column to justify receiving.

But what if I didn't need to do the math at all?

What if I could just... receive?

Not because I'd earned it. Just because I'm here. Because I'm a human being who deserves rest, kindness, beauty, love, and joy as a birthright, not a reward.

This shift didn't happen through affirmations or visualization. It happened through action. Through the practice of receiving before I felt like I'd earned it.

Through letting myself have good things even when the wound screamed I didn't deserve them yet.

Building Faith When You Can't See the Path

My grandmother had this story she told whenever I got anxious about the future.

She grew up in a small village with no electricity. When she was a girl, she'd have to walk home from her friend's house after dark, about a mile down a dirt road with no streetlights.

She only had a small lantern that illuminated maybe ten feet in front of her. The rest was complete darkness.

"I was terrified," she'd tell me. "I couldn't see the whole path. I couldn't see home. I couldn't see if there was danger ahead. All I could see was the next few steps.

"But I learned something important: I didn't need to see the whole path. I just needed to see the next few steps. And as I walked, the light moved with me. Always showing me just enough to keep going."

She'd pause here, making sure I was listening.

"Faith isn't knowing the whole path, mija. Faith is taking the next step even though you can't see beyond it. And trusting that the light will move with you."

What Faith Isn't

I spent years misunderstanding faith.

I thought faith meant being absolutely certain that things would work out exactly as I'd planned.

I thought faith meant never doubting, never questioning, never being afraid.

I thought faith meant forcing myself to believe in a specific outcome with such intensity that the universe had no choice but to deliver it.

This isn't faith. This is magical thinking with a spiritual gloss.

Real faith is so much harder. And so much more powerful.

Faith isn't the absence of doubt. It's moving forward despite the doubt.

Faith isn't knowing the outcome. It's trusting you can handle whatever comes.

Faith isn't controlling the path. It's surrendering to a wisdom larger than your own.

Faith isn't bypassing fear with positive thinking. It's feeling the fear and choosing trust anyway.

The manifestation version of faith I'd been practicing was really just control wearing a spiritual disguise. It was trying to use belief as a lever to manipulate reality into compliance with my will.

Real faith requires letting go of that control. Which feels like falling.

Learning to Fall

I learned real faith through rock climbing, of all things.

After my breakdown, I was looking for something physical, something that would get me out of my head. A friend invited me to an indoor climbing gym.

I was terrible at it. But I kept going back because something about it felt right.

One day, my instructor was teaching me to fall. There's a technique in climbing called a "trust fall" where you deliberately let go of the wall and fall backward, trusting your belayer (the person holding your rope) to catch you.

"I can't," I said, about fifteen feet up the wall. "What if they don't catch me?"

"They will," the instructor said. "But you won't know that until you let go. That's the whole point. Trust isn't proven by staying on the wall. It's proven by falling."

I stared down at my hands, white-knuckled on the holds.

"You can hold on as long as you want," she said. "But eventually, you'll get too tired and fall anyway. The question is: do you want to fall consciously, with trust? Or fall unconsciously, from exhaustion?"

I thought about how perfectly this mirrored my life. How I'd been white-knuckling everything for years, terrified of letting go, burning myself out trying to hold on.

Eventually, I was going to fall anyway. Might as well practice trust while I still had energy.

I let go.

The rope caught me. My belayer lowered me gently to the ground.

My hands were shaking. But something in me knew: I'd just learned the most important lesson.

Letting go doesn't mean crashing. It means being held.

Building the Faith Muscle

Faith isn't something you have or don't have. It's something you practice, like a muscle you strengthen over time.

Here's how I started building that muscle:

Small acts of trust. I started with tiny risks. Saying yes to an invitation without knowing everyone who'd be there. Trying a new route to work without GPS. Ordering something unfamiliar at a restaurant.

Not big leaps of faith. Small steps outside my need for total control and certainty.

Collecting evidence. I kept a "faith journal" where I wrote down every time I let go of control and things worked out anyway. Every time I didn't know the path and found it step by step. Every time I fell and was caught.

Not to manifest anything. Just to train my brain to notice: trust has been reliable. Letting go hasn't killed me yet.

Tolerating uncertainty. I practiced sitting with not-knowing. When my mind demanded answers, What's going to happen? How will this work out? What's the plan?, I'd breathe and say, "I don't know. And that's okay."

At first, this felt like drowning. The anxiety was intense.

But gradually, I learned that I could survive not-knowing. That uncertainty wasn't the enemy. That my mind's demand for certainty was just another form of control.

Trusting the process. I started noticing patterns in my own life: times when things that seemed like disasters turned out to be blessings. Rejections that led to better opportunities. Delays that turned out to be perfect timing.

I couldn't have planned any of it. But looking back, I could see the wisdom in how things unfolded.

This gave me evidence for a kind of faith that's not about controlling outcomes, but about trusting that there's an intelligence to life that's bigger than my limited perspective.

The Prayer That Changed My Life

I'm not religious, but I found myself spontaneously praying during this period. Not asking for specific outcomes. Not trying to manifest anything.

Just this simple prayer, repeated whenever I felt the grip of control taking over:

"Help me trust what I can't see. Help me let go of what I can't control. Help me receive what's trying to reach me."

That's it. Not a demand. Not a negotiation. Not a manifestation formula.

Just a humble acknowledgment: I can't do this alone. I don't have all the answers. I need to trust something bigger than my own will.

Some people call that something God. Some call it the universe. Some call it the intelligence of life itself.

I don't care what you call it. What matters is the posture: releasing control and opening to trust.

This prayer didn't make my life easier. It didn't make things happen faster. It didn't give me certainty or control.

But it gave me peace in the uncertainty. It gave me the ability to keep going even when I couldn't see the path. It gave me faith, real faith, not the fake certainty kind, that I would be okay even if things didn't go according to plan.

Where I Am Now

I still don't know what's coming. I still can't see the whole path.

But I've learned to walk with just the lantern light that illuminates the next few steps. And to trust that as I walk, the light moves with me.

I still have desires. Still have dreams. Still move toward things I want to create and experience.

But I hold them differently now. With open hands instead of clenched fists. With curiosity instead of control. With trust instead of force.

And the strangest thing has happened: the more I let go of the timeline, the less attached I am to specific outcomes, the more willing I am to walk in the dark, the more things seem to flow toward me.

Not because I've finally mastered manifestation. But because I've finally stopped strangling everything with my grip.

The river was always trying to carry me home. I just had to stop fighting it and let it.

PRACTICE: THE DESERVING EXERCISE

Here's a practice that helped me shift from earning to deserving:

Part 1: Notice the Calculation

For one week, pay attention to how often you do this mental math: Have I earned this? Do I deserve this yet?

Notice it when you're deciding whether to rest. Whether to treat yourself to something nice. Whether to say no. Whether to receive a compliment.

Just notice the calculation. Don't judge it. Just see how automatic it is.

Part 2: Receive Without Earning

Every day this week, do one thing that feels good without earning it first.

Sleep in without working late the night before.
Buy yourself flowers without accomplishing anything

special.
Take a break without finishing your to-do list first.
Accept a compliment without deflecting or explaining.

Notice the discomfort. Notice the wound screaming that you haven't earned this yet. Notice the guilt, the anxiety, the sense that you're being selfish.

And do it anyway.

This is how you build the deserving muscle. Not through affirmations, but through action. Through the radical practice of receiving good things just because you exist.

Part 3: The Trust Walk

Once this week, do something without knowing the outcome.

Take a walk without a destination in mind, just wander and see where you end up.
Start a creative project without planning what it will become.
Have a conversation without an agenda for where it should go.

Practice the lantern-light faith: just the next step, not the whole path.

Notice what happens when you stop trying to control the destination and just trust the journey.

You might be surprised by where you end up. Or more likely, you'll be surprised by how much lighter you feel when you finally stop trying to carry the weight of the whole unknown future.

PART SIX: FROM CHASER TO MAGNET

The Energy Shift That Changes Everything

Why "High Vibe" Culture Is Making You Exhausted

I met Vanessa at a manifestation retreat in Sedona. She was the person everyone wanted to sit next to during meals, always smiling, always positive, always radiating what the retreat leader kept calling "high-vibe energy."

"I'm just so blessed," she'd say, eyes sparkling. "Everything is always working out for my highest good. I'm so grateful for this abundant universe."

She posted inspirational quotes on Instagram every morning. Her feed was all sunrise yoga poses and green smoothies and captions about staying in your frequency. She never complained. Never admitted struggle. Never let the mask slip.

On the third night of the retreat, I found her crying in the bathroom.

Not delicate tears. Full-body sobs, the kind that come from something breaking inside you.

"Are you okay?" I asked, which was stupid because obviously she wasn't.

She looked up at me, mascara streaking down her face, and something in her just... cracked open.

"I'm so fucking tired," she whispered. "I'm so tired of being positive all the time. Of monitoring my vibration every second. Of being afraid to feel anything real because it might lower my frequency. I haven't cried in two years because crying is 'low vibe.' I haven't been honest about my life in two years because struggling means you're not manifesting correctly. I'm exhausted from performing happiness while I'm dying inside."

She told me about her real life. The marriage that was falling apart. The financial stress she was drowning in. The anxiety that woke her up at 3 AM every night. The depression she couldn't admit to because admitting it would mean she was doing manifestation wrong.

"The retreat leader said if we're not happy, it's because we're choosing low-vibe thoughts," she said. "So I smile. I post my gratitude lists. I say everything is amazing. And I hate myself a little more every day for being such a failure at this."

I sat down on the bathroom floor next to her. "You're not a failure. The system is failing you."

The High-Vibe Tyranny

"High vibe" has become the spiritual equivalent of "thoughts and prayers", something people say that sounds meaningful but ultimately leaves you more alone with your pain.

The message is everywhere: Stay positive. Keep your vibration high. Don't let anything bring you down. Surround yourself only with high-vibe people, high-vibe foods, high-vibe content. Anything less and you're attracting negativity.

It sounds empowering. Like you're taking control of your energy, your reality, your life.

But here's what it actually does: it makes you terrified of your own humanity.

Because humans have a full range of emotions. We get sad. We get angry. We get scared. We grieve, worry, doubt, and sometimes fall apart. This isn't a bug in the system, it's the system working correctly. Emotions are information. They tell us what matters. They help us process life. They connect us to each other through shared experience.

But high-vibe culture has rebranded normal human emotions as dangerous. As things to be avoided, suppressed, or "transmuted" as quickly as possible.

Feeling sad? Better shift that energy quick before you attract more sadness.
Feeling angry? That's definitely low vibe, go do some gratitude journaling.
Feeling scared? You're blocking your manifestations with fear-based thinking.
Feeling anything other than joy, peace, and abundant gratitude? You're doing it wrong.

This isn't wellness. This is emotional bypass with a vision board.

What "High Vibe" Actually Costs You

I spent eighteen months trying to stay perpetually high-vibe. Here's what it cost me:

Authenticity. I became a walking Instagram caption. "Living my best life!" "So blessed!" "Everything is working out!" Meanwhile, I was having panic attacks in parking lots and crying myself to sleep.

Connection. I cut off anyone who was going through a hard time because their "energy was bringing me down." I lost real friends who needed support because I was afraid their problems would lower my vibration.

Emotional resilience. I never learned how to actually process difficult emotions because I was too busy trying to positive-think my way out of them. So they just accumulated in my body, creating more anxiety, more stress, more of the very low-vibe energy I was trying to avoid.

Self-trust. Every time I felt something other than positive, I thought something was wrong with me. I became so disconnected from my actual feelings that I couldn't tell the difference between my intuition and my anxiety anymore.

Energy. The irony: trying to stay high-vibe all the time was the most depleting thing I've ever done. It takes enormous energy to perform constant happiness. To police every thought and feeling. To maintain a facade of perpetual positivity.

Humanity. I became less human, less real, less alive. I was a well-curated spiritual Instagram account with no actual person behind it.

And the sickest part? I was doing all of this because I thought it would make me more attractive, more magnetic, more capable of manifesting what I wanted.

But you know what's actually magnetic? Being real.

What Actually Makes You Magnetic

My nephew is four years old. His name is Leo, and he's the most magnetic person I know.

Not because he's always happy, he has epic meltdowns at least twice a week. Not because he's always positive, yesterday he told me my cooking "tastes like garbage" with brutal honesty. Not because he controls his vibration, he feels every emotion at full volume and expresses it completely.

He's magnetic because he's fully himself. Unfiltered. Authentic. Present.

When he's happy, he's all-the-way happy. Spinning in circles, laughing from his belly, infectious joy that makes everyone around him smile.

When he's sad, he's all-the-way sad. Big tears, genuine grief, no pretending or minimizing.

When he's curious, he asks seventeen questions in a row until he understands.

When he's mad, he lets you know. Then five minutes later, he's forgotten all about it and wants to play trains.

People are drawn to him. Not because he's performing being delightful. But because he's authentic in a world full of performance. Because you always know where you stand with him. Because his presence isn't manufactured, it's just him.

This is what actually makes you magnetic: being unapologetically yourself.

The Magnetism Research

After my high-vibe burnout, I got curious about what actually attracts people to each other. Not in a romantic sense, but in a general "I want to be around this person" sense.

I read studies on charisma, on influence, on what makes some people naturally draw others in. And the findings were consistent:

Authenticity is more attractive than perfection. People who show vulnerability, who admit mistakes, who are real about their struggles, they're more likable, more trustworthy, more magnetic than people who present a perfect facade.

There's even a name for it: the "pratfall effect." People who are competent but occasionally screw up are more appealing than people who never make mistakes. Because perfection is intimidating. Humanity is relatable.

Presence is more attractive than performance. People who are actually listening, actually engaged, actually here, they're magnetic. People who are half-present while monitoring their own performance aren't.

Emotional range is more attractive than constant positivity. People who can feel the full spectrum, who can cry at weddings and laugh at funerals and get angry at injustice and be tender with pain, they're more real, more trustworthy, more human than people who only show one emotional note.

Groundedness is more attractive than spiritual bypassing. People who can acknowledge difficulty without being consumed by it, who can hold pain without drowning in it, who can be real about their struggles while still moving forward, that's magnetic.

None of this has anything to do with maintaining a high vibration. It's all about being genuinely yourself.

The Magnet I Met in a Coffee Shop

There was this woman who came into my neighborhood coffee shop every Tuesday morning. I started noticing her because everyone else did too.

She wasn't conventionally beautiful. She didn't dress like an Instagram influencer. She didn't have perfect posture or radiant skin or any of the things high-vibe culture says you need.

But she was magnetic. Baristas lit up when she came in. Other customers gravitated toward her. Strangers struck up conversations with her in line.

One day, I asked her directly. "What's your secret? People are just drawn to you."

She laughed, a real laugh, not a performed one. "No secret. I just show up as myself. Some days that's cheerful, some days it's tired. Some days I'm chatty, some days I barely speak. I stopped trying to be anything other than whatever I am that day."

"But doesn't that... I don't know, bring your energy down sometimes? Being tired or quiet?"

She gave me this look, kind but penetrating. "Energy isn't about always being 'up.' It's about being real. People can feel the difference between someone who's genuinely peaceful and someone who's performing peace. Between someone who's authentically joyful and someone who's forcing themselves to smile because they think they have to."

She paused, then added, "The most magnetic people I've ever met weren't the ones who were always positive. They were the ones who were always honest."

The Difference Between Authentic Frequency and Fake Positivity

After my conversation with the coffee shop woman, I started paying attention to the difference between people who felt genuinely good to be around and people who felt exhausting despite their positivity.

I realized there were two completely different types of energy:

Authentic frequency: This is who you actually are when you stop performing. It's your natural state when you're not trying to be anything. It fluctuates based on what you're experiencing, what you need, where you are in your life. Sometimes it's high, sometimes it's low, sometimes it's neutral. But it's always real.

Fake positivity: This is the performance of being fine. The mask of spiritual bypassing. The forced smile and the scripted "I'm so blessed!" when you're actually falling apart. It's exhausting to maintain and exhausting to be around.

Here's how to tell the difference:

Authentic Frequency

Feels like: Being around someone who makes you feel like you can breathe. Who doesn't need you to be anything other than what you are. Who creates space for real conversation, real feeling, real presence.

Sounds like:
"I'm having a hard week, but I'm working through it."
"That was really disappointing. I need to sit with this feeling for a bit."
"I don't know how I feel about that yet. Let me think about it."
"I'm genuinely happy right now. This feels good."

Looks like: Congruence. Their words match their body language match their energy. When they say they're fine, they actually seem fine. When they say they're struggling, you can see it.

Creates: Connection, trust, realness. You feel safe being yourself around them because they're being themselves.

Fake Positivity

Feels like: Being around someone who needs you to help them maintain their illusion. Who gets uncomfortable if you're not also being positive. Who creates an unspoken pressure to perform happiness.

Sounds like:
"Everything happens for a reason!" (said while clearly in pain)
"I'm so blessed!" (said like a mantra to ward off reality)
"Only good vibes!" (said to shut down any real conversation)
"I'm choosing not to let that affect me." (said while clearly affected)

Looks like: Dissonance. Their words say one thing but their body says another. Forced smile that doesn't reach their eyes. Tight shoulders while claiming to be relaxed. Agitation while insisting everything is amazing.

Creates: Distance, performance anxiety, loneliness. You feel like you have to hide parts of yourself to be acceptable to them.

My Authentic Frequency Experiment

After Sedona, after that bathroom conversation with Vanessa, I decided to run an experiment: What if I stopped trying to be high-vibe and just let myself be... whatever I was?

Monday: Tired. I was tired. So instead of forcing myself to be energetic and upbeat, I just told people "I'm a bit low-energy today" when they asked how I was. Revolutionary.

Tuesday: Irritable. Instead of doing gratitude journaling to shift the irritability, I acknowledged it. "I'm feeling cranky today and I don't know why." Then I went for a run, which helped more than any affirmation ever had.

Wednesday: Genuinely happy. Something good happened at work and I felt light, joyful. I let myself feel it without analyzing whether I was "in the right vibration" or trying to manufacture more of it.

Thursday: Sad. A friend was going through something hard and it affected me. Instead of trying to transmute the sadness, I let myself cry. Then I called her and we cried together. It was real. It was connecting. It was more healing than any high-vibe practice I'd ever done.

Friday: Peaceful. A quiet, grounded peace. Not manufactured. Just there.

The most surprising thing? People responded better to me. Way better.

When I was tired and said so, people were kind. They related. They shared their own tiredness. We connected over being human together.

When I was sad and let it show, people held space for me. Real space, not the "let's shift your energy" kind.

When I was genuinely happy, people felt it. Because it was real, not performed.

The authentic frequency, even when it wasn't "high", was more magnetic than all my forced positivity had ever been.

How to Attract Instead of Chase

My friend Marcus teaches ballroom dancing. I took his class once, thinking it might be fun. It was harder than I expected.

"You're working too hard," he told me during a waltz. "You're trying to lead when you're supposed to follow. But also, you're chasing your partner instead of moving with them."

"I don't understand the difference," I said.

He stopped the music. "When you chase, you're leaning forward, anticipating, trying to control where we're going. You're ahead of the music, ahead of me, ahead of yourself. It creates tension. Makes everything harder."

"And when I'm moving with you?"

"You're right here. Present with me, with the music, with the movement. You're responsive instead of controlling. That's when the dance flows. That's when it's actually enjoyable instead of exhausting."

He started the music again. "Stop chasing. Just be here. Move with me."

Something clicked. I stopped trying to anticipate every step. Stopped trying to control the direction. Just followed the lead, listened to the music, stayed present with the movement.

The dance became effortless. Beautiful, even.

"There it is," Marcus said. "That's the difference. Chasing is exhausting. Dancing is magnetic."

The Energy of Chasing vs. Attracting

I thought about this dance lesson for weeks. Because it perfectly illustrated what I'd been doing wrong in every area of my life.

Chasing energy:

- Leaning forward into the future
- Trying to control the outcome
- Anticipating, planning, forcing
- Ahead of yourself, never present
- Tense, effortful, exhausting
- Pushes things away through desperation

Attracting energy:

- Grounded in the present moment
- Trusting the process
- Responsive, flowing, allowing
- Right here, fully engaged
- Relaxed, easeful, sustainable
- Draws things in through magnetic presence

I'd been chasing everything. Jobs, relationships, money, healing, growth. Always leaning forward, never here. Always trying to control the next step instead of being fully present with this one.

And chasing is repelling. People can feel it. Opportunities can sense it. Life resists it.

But when you're fully present, fully yourself, fully here, that's magnetic.

What I Stopped Doing

To shift from chaser to magnet, I had to stop doing things that created chasing energy:

Stopped checking. I deleted the apps that let me check my bank account seventeen times a day, check if he'd texted back, check if anyone liked my post. All that checking was just anxious chasing disguised as awareness.

Stopped performing. I stopped curating my life for an audience. Stopped posting only the highlights. Stopped pretending everything was amazing when it wasn't. Stopped being who I thought I should be.

Stopped forcing. When I noticed myself pushing, controlling, trying to make something happen, I'd stop. Breathe. Ask: what wants to happen here naturally? Then let it.

Stopped fixing. I stopped trying to fix every difficult emotion immediately. Stopped reaching for a technique or practice every time I felt uncomfortable. Started just being with what is.

Stopped comparing. I stopped measuring my progress against anyone else's timeline. Stopped checking to see if I was "further along" than I was last month. Just let myself be exactly where I was.

Each thing I stopped doing created more space. More presence. More groundedness.

More magnetism.

What I Started Doing

And I started doing things that created attracting energy:

Started showing up fully. Whatever energy I had that day, that's what I brought. Tired? Brought tired. Excited? Brought excited. Unsure? Brought unsure. No more performing a version of myself.

Started listening. Really listening. To people, to my body, to the moment. Not half-listening while planning what to say next or checking if this was aligned with my goals.

Started being where I was. If I was washing dishes, I washed dishes. If I was having coffee with a friend, I had coffee with a friend. No more being physically present while mentally somewhere else.

Started trusting my response. Instead of overthinking every decision, I started trusting my immediate felt response. Does this feel like a yes or a no? Then that's my answer.

Started appreciating what's here. Not forced gratitude practice. Just genuine noticing of what's already good. The sun on my face. The friend who texted. The fact that I can walk, breathe, think, feel.

None of this is complicated. But it completely changed my energy from chasing to attracting.

The Job That Found Me

The clearest example of this shift came with my current work.

For months, I'd been desperately job hunting. Sending out resumes, networking frantically, checking LinkedIn obsessively. Classic chasing energy. And nothing was landing.

Then I stopped. Not gave up, just stopped chasing. I focused on being present with my current (not ideal but okay) situation. Started actually connecting with colleagues instead of treating them as networking opportunities. Started doing my current work well instead of mentally being somewhere else.

One day, my colleague Sarah asked if I wanted to grab lunch. Normally I would have said no, I didn't see how lunch with Sarah advanced my goals. But I was practicing presence, so I said yes.

We talked about nothing important. Her weekend plans. A show she was watching. Her sister's wedding.

Then, almost as an afterthought: "Oh, my friend runs a nonprofit that's hiring. I thought of you because you'd be perfect for it. Want me to introduce you?"

I got that job. Not through strategic networking or aggressive job hunting. Through being present with someone, connecting genuinely, and letting the opportunity find me.

That's the difference. Chasing pushes opportunities away. Presence attracts them.

The Practice of Being Magnetic

Here's what I learned about magnetism: it's not something you do. It's something you stop preventing.

You're naturally magnetic. You were magnetic as a child, before you learned to perform, to people-please, to hide your truth to be acceptable.

The work isn't becoming magnetic. It's removing everything that's blocking your natural magnetism.

Remove the performance. Stop trying to be who you think you should be. Stop curating yourself for an audience. Just be who you are.

Remove the chasing. Stop leaning into the future. Stop trying to control outcomes. Come back to right here, right now.

Remove the fake positivity. Stop forcing yourself to be happy when you're not. Stop bypassing real emotions with spiritual platitudes. Feel what you feel.

Remove the comparison. Stop measuring yourself against anyone else. Your journey is yours. Their timeline is irrelevant.

Remove the trying. Stop working so hard to be magnetic. Stop strategizing your energy. Just be.

What's left when you remove all that? You. The real you. The you that people are actually drawn to.

That's the magnet. That's what attracts. Not the performed version. The real one.

PRACTICE: THE AUTHENTICITY AUDIT

Here's an exercise that helped me shift from chaser to magnet:

Part 1: Notice Your Performance

For three days, pay attention to when you're performing vs. when you're being real.

Notice when you say you're fine when you're not.
Notice when you force enthusiasm you don't feel.
Notice when you curate your answer to seem more positive, spiritual, or together than you are.
Notice when you're being who you think you should be instead of who you are.

Just notice. No judgment. Just awareness.

Part 2: Tell One Truth

Each day, tell one authentic truth you'd normally hide.

"I'm actually feeling pretty low today."
"I don't know if I agree with that."
"That hurt my feelings."
"I'm genuinely happy about this."

Start small. Low stakes. But practice authenticity.

Part 3: The Presence Practice

Once a day, be fully present with whatever you're doing.

If you're drinking coffee, just drink coffee. Taste it. Feel the warmth.
If you're talking to someone, actually listen. Stop planning your response.
If you're walking, feel your feet on the ground. Notice your surroundings.

Just five minutes of genuine presence. No phone. No multitasking. No being mentally somewhere else.

Notice how it feels to stop chasing the next moment and actually be in this one.

This is what makes you magnetic: being here. Being real. Being you.

Not the high-vibe version. Not the perfect version. Not the version you think you should be.

Just you. Right here. Right now. Fully present and unapologetically real.

That's the magnet. That's what attracts everything worth having.

PART SEVEN: RELEASING IN REAL LIFE

Money, Love, Work, and Health

The Scarcity Death Spiral: Letting Go of Financial Desperation

I'll never forget the afternoon I spent $47 on a "money manifestation crystal" while I had $53 in my bank account and rent due in five days.

The irony wasn't lost on me even as I was handing over my debit card. Here I was, desperately broke, spending money I didn't have on a rock that was supposed to attract abundance. The shopkeeper wrapped it in special paper and told me to sleep with it under my pillow and visualize wealth flowing to me.

I did exactly that. For three nights, I clutched that crystal, visualized money, affirmed abundance, and woke up just as broke as when I'd fallen asleep, only now with even less money because I'd bought the damn crystal.

On the fourth morning, I threw the crystal across the room. It didn't break, of course it didn't, I'd paid extra for "premium grade", but something in me did.

I called my grandmother. "Abuela, I don't understand. I'm doing everything the manifestation teachers say. Why am I still broke?"

She was quiet for a moment. Then: "Mija, tell me something. When you think about money, what do you feel?"

"I feel... scared. Panicked. Like there's never enough and there never will be."

"And when you do your manifestation practices?"

"I try to feel abundant. Like money is flowing to me easily."

"But do you actually feel that?"

I paused. "No. I feel like I'm lying to myself. Like I'm pretending to feel abundant while I'm terrified."

"So you're practicing fear with a smile on your face."

That hit me like a truck. She was right. Every manifestation practice I did around money was just fear in disguise. Desperate fear dressed up as spiritual practice.

What Desperation Actually Does

Here's what I learned about financial desperation: it doesn't just feel bad. It actively pushes money away.

Not because of some mystical vibration nonsense. Because of how it affects your decision-making, your behavior, your entire relationship with resources.

When you're desperate for money, you make terrible financial decisions. You say yes to jobs that underpay you because you're scared you won't get anything better. You spend money you don't have on things that promise quick fixes. You can't negotiate because you're terrified they'll walk away. You can't walk away from bad situations because you're convinced nothing else will come.

I watched this play out in my own life for years.

I stayed at a job that paid me $15,000 below market rate because I was afraid if I asked for more, they'd fire me. I bought every manifestation course that promised to solve my money problems, going deeper into debt trying to manifest my way out of debt. I couldn't turn down freelance work even when it paid terribly because "money is money."

The desperation kept me stuck in scarcity. Not because I wasn't manifesting correctly. Because I was making fear-based choices.

The Day I Stopped Clutching

The shift came when I had exactly $1,200 in my account. Enough to cover rent with $150 left over.

A friend invited me to a concert. Tickets were $80. The old me would have immediately calculated: if I spend $80, I'll only have $70 left for the rest of the month. Too risky. Can't do it.

But I was practicing this letting-go thing. So I asked myself a different question: What would I do if I trusted money to keep flowing?

The answer was immediate: I'd go to the concert.

So I did. I bought the ticket. Not recklessly, I wasn't going into debt for it. But I chose to trust that $70 would be enough, that more money would come, that I didn't have to death-grip every dollar out of fear.

That weekend, I ran into someone at the concert. We got talking. Turns out she ran a small marketing agency and was looking for a freelance writer. She hired me the following week. That contract brought in $3,000 over the next month.

Now, I don't think the universe magically rewarded me for buying concert tickets. That's not how this works.

What happened was: when I stopped operating from desperate scarcity, I was present enough to have a real conversation. I wasn't radiating "please hire me I'm broke" energy. I was just a person enjoying music who happened to have skills someone needed.

The clutching had been making me desperate and weird. The releasing made me available for opportunity.

The Wallet Meditation

After that experience, I started doing what I called the "wallet meditation." Not a real meditation, just a practice.

Every time I felt panic about money, every time I wanted to clutch and control and desperately strategize, I'd physically open my wallet. Look at whatever money was there, whether it was $5 or $500.

Then I'd say out loud: "This is enough for right now. More will come when I need it."

At first, this felt insane. Like lying. How could $5 be enough? How could I trust more would come?

But I kept doing it. And slowly, something shifted.

I stopped checking my bank account seventeen times a day. I stopped panicking every time an unexpected expense came up. I stopped making decisions purely from fear of running out.

And weirdly, I don't fully understand this even now, my financial situation started improving. Not dramatically. Not overnight. But steadily.

I started getting better-paying work. I started saying no to underpaid projects, which created space for better ones. I started negotiating, which I'd never had the courage to do before. I started seeing opportunities I'd been too panicked to notice.

The less I clutched money, the more it seemed to flow.

Love Without Needing: Attracting from Wholeness

Two years before I met my now-partner, I was absolutely convinced I'd found "the one."

His name was David. He was smart, successful, shared my interests, looked good on paper. I was sure the universe had sent him to me as a reward for all my manifestation work.

There was just one problem: he was emotionally unavailable, occasionally cruel, and made it very clear he didn't want a relationship.

But I'd manifested him! He matched my list! He had to be the one!

So I stayed. For eight months, I stayed. Making myself smaller, quieter, less needy. Convincing myself that if I just loved him hard enough, if I just proved my worth enough, he'd change his mind.

I journaled about him constantly. I visualized us together. I did cord-cutting rituals when he pulled away, then immediately visualized the cords reforming because I wanted him back. I read his texts like tea leaves, looking for hidden meanings, signs that he was coming around.

My friends were gentle at first. "Sofia, this doesn't seem healthy."

Then less gentle. "He's literally telling you he doesn't want a relationship. Why won't you listen?"

I didn't listen because I needed it to work. I'd invested so much, emotionally, energetically, spiritually. If this didn't work out, what did that say about my manifestation abilities? What did it say about me?

Looking back, I can see it clearly: I wasn't in love with David. I was in love with not being alone. I was in love with the idea of having manifested my person. I was in love with proving that I was lovable.

I didn't want David. I needed him. And need is the opposite of love.

When I Finally Let Go

It ended on a random Tuesday. We were supposed to meet for coffee. He cancelled last minute, again, with a vague excuse.

And instead of the usual spiral of "what did I do wrong, how can I fix this, maybe I should text him something cute," I just... stopped.

I sat there with my cancelled plans and my cooling coffee and I felt something shift. Not a dramatic breakthrough. Just a quiet knowing: I'm done.

Not done with him specifically. Done with needing someone, anyone, to validate my worth. Done with contorting myself to fit someone else's limited capacity. Done with calling desperation "love."

I texted him: "I don't think this is working for me anymore. I wish you well."

He didn't respond for three days. When he did, it was a long message about how he valued me and wasn't ready to lose me and maybe we could try again.

The old me would have been elated. See? He does care! It's working!

The new me read it clearly: he doesn't want me. He just doesn't want to lose the attention.

I didn't respond.

The Wholeness Experiment

After David, I did something radical: I decided to be done with dating for six months. Not because I was giving up on love. Because I needed to figure out who I was when I wasn't trying to be someone's girlfriend.

I'd been dating, or trying to date, or pining after someone, since I was fourteen. I'd never just been alone. My entire sense of self was wrapped up in whether someone wanted me.

Those six months were uncomfortable. I had to sit with feelings I'd been avoiding by staying busy with relationship drama. Loneliness. Fear that I was unlovable. Boredom with my own company.

But I also discovered things I'd forgotten about myself.

I actually enjoyed my own company. I was funny when I wasn't monitoring whether someone else found me funny. I had opinions I'd been hiding to seem agreeable. I had interests I'd abandoned to match someone else's.

I started doing things just because I wanted to, not because they'd make good date stories. I took a pottery class. Started cooking elaborate meals just for myself. Went to movies alone. Traveled to a cabin in the woods for a weekend and just... existed.

And somewhere in those six months, something fundamental shifted: I stopped feeling like half of something waiting for the other half to appear. I started feeling whole.

Not in a "I don't need anyone" toxic independence way. I still wanted partnership. But I wanted it as an addition to my life, not as the foundation of my life.

Meeting Marcus

I met Marcus on month seven. At a friend's birthday party. I wasn't looking for anyone, genuinely wasn't. I was just there to celebrate my friend.

We ended up talking for three hours. About books, about our families, about this ridiculous conspiracy theory his uncle believed about pigeons being government drones.

At the end of the night, he asked for my number. I gave it to him, but I wasn't desperate about it. If he called, great. If not, I'd had a nice conversation and would continue being perfectly fine.

He called. We went out. And it was... easy.

Not in a "this is effortless and perfect" way. In a "this is two whole people choosing to spend time together" way.

I didn't contort myself to be what he wanted because I already liked who I was. He didn't need me to complete him because he was already complete. We added to each other's lives instead of filling holes in each other.

The difference between this and every relationship before was striking. With David and all the others, I'd been trying to get them to love me into wholeness. With Marcus, I came whole and invited him to be whole with me.

That's the difference between needing and loving. Need is trying to extract wholeness from someone else. Love is offering wholeness and receiving it in return.

Career Without Clutching: Finding Your Path by Releasing the Plan

For five years, I had a very specific career plan mapped out.

By 25: Marketing coordinator at a mid-size company.
By 27: Marketing manager.
By 30: Director of Marketing.
By 35: VP of Marketing at a major corporation, six-figure salary, corner office, the works.

I had the trajectory. I had the milestones. I had everything planned down to which companies I'd target at each stage.

What I didn't have was any sense of whether this was what I actually wanted. I'd built this plan when I was 22, fresh out of college, trying to prove I was ambitious and successful and on track.

I never stopped to ask: On track to what? And do I even want to go there?

The Career Crisis

At 28, I got the manager position. Right on schedule. I should have been thrilled.

Instead, I was miserable. The job was exactly what I'd planned for, and it felt completely wrong. I spent my days in meetings that could have been emails, managing people who resented being managed, hitting arbitrary metrics that meant nothing to me.

I cried in my car during lunch breaks. I dreaded Sunday evenings. I felt like I was slowly suffocating in a life that looked successful from the outside but felt hollow from the inside.

But I couldn't leave. This was the plan. I'd worked so hard to get here. If I left, what did that say about me? That I was a quitter? That I couldn't handle success?

Plus, I'd already told everyone this was my dream job. How could I admit I was wrong?

So I stayed. For two years. Getting more and more depleted. Making myself sick with stress. Convinced I just needed to try harder to appreciate what I had.

The Permission Slip I Didn't Know I Needed

The breaking point came during a performance review.

My boss was praising me, telling me I was on track for director within two years. "You're exactly where you should be," she said.

And I burst into tears. Right there in her office.

"What's wrong?" she asked, genuinely confused.

"I don't want to be a director," I heard myself say. "I don't want any of this."

The admission felt like falling. Like admitting I'd wasted years working toward something I didn't actually want.

But also, relief. Enormous, overwhelming relief.

She was kinder than I expected. "What do you want to do?"

"I have no idea," I said. And it was true. I'd been following the plan for so long I'd lost touch with my actual desires.

That conversation changed everything. Not because she gave me permission, I didn't need her permission. But because I finally gave myself permission to not know. To admit the plan wasn't working. To release my death grip on a future that wasn't even mine.

Finding the Path by Losing the Map

I quit three months later. No backup plan. No new job lined up. Just a clear knowing that I couldn't spend one more day pretending this was working.

Everyone thought I was insane. My mother cried. My friends asked what my plan was. My former colleagues looked at me like I'd lost my mind.

"What are you going to do?" everyone kept asking.

"I don't know yet," I'd say. And watch them get uncomfortable with my uncertainty.

But I'd learned something from all my releasing practice: sometimes the only way to find the right path is to get off the wrong one. Even when you can't see the next path yet.

I gave myself six months to explore. To try things. To say yes to opportunities that sounded interesting even if they didn't "make sense" for my career.

I did some freelance writing. Took a part-time job at a nonprofit just to pay bills. Volunteered at the grief center where I'd been going for my own processing. Started teaching a workshop about letting go.

None of it was strategic. I wasn't building toward anything. I was just following what felt alive.

And six months later, someone who'd taken my workshop reached out. She ran a retreat center and wanted to know if I'd design a program about release and transformation.

I said yes, not because it fit a plan, but because it excited me.

That led to another program. Then another. Then a training in grief work. Then a practice working with people in transition.

Five years later, I'm doing work I never could have planned for because it didn't exist in my awareness when I was 22 making that career map. I help people navigate transitions, release what's not working, and find their way forward without having to know the whole path.

It's not what I planned. It's so much better than what I planned.

But I only found it by releasing the plan.

Your Body's Wisdom: Healing Through Trust, Not Force

I spent my twenties at war with my body.

It was too heavy. Too tired. Too anxious. Too sensitive. It had chronic pain I couldn't explain and digestive issues that baffled doctors and migraines that came out of nowhere and panic attacks that made no sense.

So I tried to fix it. Through sheer force of will.

I did elimination diets, cutting out entire food groups. I took dozens of supplements. I tried every healing modality: acupuncture, chiropractors, energy work, naturopaths. I exercised aggressively to "burn out" the anxiety. I meditated to force my nervous system to calm down. I journaled to release trauma. I did breathwork until I hyperventilated.

I approached healing like a military campaign. If I just worked hard enough, tried enough things, controlled every variable, surely my body would comply.

It didn't. If anything, I got worse.

The Migraine That Taught Me Everything

The worst migraine of my life came the day after an intense healing workshop where we'd done six hours of trauma release work.

I woke up with pain so severe I couldn't open my eyes. Couldn't move. Couldn't think. Just blinding, nauseating pain.

I tried everything in my arsenal. Ice. Heat. Medication. Essential oils. Acupressure. Affirmations. Visualizing the pain leaving my body. Asking my higher self what I needed to learn from this.

Nothing worked. The migraine lasted for three days.

On the third day, exhausted and defeated, I stopped trying to fix it. I couldn't fix it. Nothing I did made any difference.

So I just... lay there. Surrendered to it. Stopped fighting.

And in that surrender, something shifted. Not the pain, that was still there. But my relationship to it.

I started listening instead of fighting. What is this pain trying to tell me?

The answer came quietly: You're pushing too hard. You're trying to force healing the same way you forced everything else. Your body needs rest, not another healing technique.

I started crying. Because it was true. I'd been attacking my body's problems with the same aggressive energy that created them in the first place.

Learning My Body's Language

After that migraine, I started paying attention differently.

Not "what's wrong with me and how do I fix it?" but "what is my body trying to communicate?"

The chronic pain in my shoulders? "You're carrying too much. Put something down."

The digestive issues? "You're anxious about something you won't admit. What are you afraid to digest?"

The exhaustion? "You need rest. Real rest. Not productive rest or self-care that's actually another to-do item. Actual rest."

The anxiety? "You're not safe yet. Something needs to change."

When I stopped trying to make the symptoms go away and started listening to what they were telling me, everything shifted.

The shoulder pain led me to realize I was saying yes to too many obligations. When I started saying no, the pain eased.

The digestive issues led me to recognize I was in a toxic work environment. When I quit, my gut healed.

The exhaustion led me to see I was running on stress hormones and caffeine instead of actual energy. When I started sleeping properly and reducing my obligations, I had energy again.

The anxiety led me to understand my nervous system was stuck in threat mode from years of forcing and controlling. When I started doing gentle, regulating practices instead of aggressive healing, the anxiety softened.

The Body Trust Practice

Now I have a completely different relationship with my body. Instead of treating it like a broken machine I need to fix, I treat it like a wise adviser I need to listen to.

When something hurts, I ask: What are you trying to tell me?

When I'm exhausted, I ask: What do you need?

When symptoms appear, I ask: What am I not paying attention to?

And then, this is the hard part, I trust the answers.

If my body says rest, I rest. Even when my mind says there's too much to do.

If my body says no, I say no. Even when saying yes would be easier.

If my body says move, I move. Even when I'd rather stay on the couch.

This isn't about following every whim. It's about treating my body as an intelligent system that knows things my conscious mind doesn't.

And the healing that's come from this trust is deeper and more lasting than anything I achieved through force.

REFLECTION: Where Are You Clutching?

Look at these four areas: money, love, work, health.

Where are you gripping? Where are you trying to force? Where are you operating from desperation instead of trust?

Money: Are you making decisions from fear of not having enough? Or from trust that enough will come?

Love: Are you trying to get someone to love you into wholeness? Or offering your wholeness to someone else who's whole?

Work: Are you clutching a plan that stopped serving you years ago? Or following what's actually alive for you now?

Health: Are you fighting your body? Or listening to it?

The answer isn't to fix these things. The answer is to notice where you're clutching and practice, just practice, releasing the grip.

Not all at once. Not perfectly. Just a little bit of release in one area.

And see what becomes possible when you finally let go.

PART EIGHT: THE PAST, THE FUTURE, AND NOW

Releasing What Was and What Could Be

The Weight of Yesterday That's Blocking Tomorrow

My father left when I was seven. Just walked out one Tuesday morning and never came back. No explanation. No goodbye. Just gone.

For the next twenty-three years, I carried that Tuesday morning with me everywhere. It colored every relationship. Shaped every decision. Whispered in my ear during every moment of happiness: "This won't last. People leave. Don't get comfortable."

I didn't realize I was doing this. I thought I'd dealt with it. I'd been to therapy. I'd forgiven him, or so I told myself. I'd done the inner child work and the father wound healing and read all the books about daughters of absent fathers.

But the past doesn't let go just because you've intellectually processed it. It stays in your body. In your patterns. In the way you unconsciously organize your entire life around making sure that Tuesday morning never happens again.

The Pattern I Couldn't See

I had this thing I did in relationships. About three months in, right when things were getting good, I'd start picking fights. Not consciously. But I'd find things to be upset about. Small things that I'd blow up into big things.

"You didn't text me back for three hours. Do you even care about this relationship?"

"You made plans without asking me first. I guess I'm not a priority."

"You seem distant lately. Are you losing interest?"

Every guy I dated would eventually say some version of the same thing: "I feel like you're waiting for me to leave. Like you're testing me to see when I'll give up."

And I'd get defensive. "I'm not testing anyone! I just have standards! I just know what I deserve!"

But they were right. I was testing them. Unconsciously pushing them to see if they'd stay. Trying to control the inevitable abandonment by making it happen on my terms instead of being blindsided like I was at seven.

The past was running my present. And I couldn't see it because I was inside it.

The Confrontation I Needed

It was my friend Rachel who finally called me on it.

We were having coffee and I was complaining about my latest almost-relationship that had just ended. "I don't get it. Why do I keep attracting emotionally unavailable men?"

Rachel set down her cup. "Sofia, can I be honest with you? Really honest?"

"Of course."

"You don't attract emotionally unavailable men. You attract perfectly available men and then push them away the moment they get too close. You've done it with the last five guys. Maybe more."

I felt my defenses rise. "That's not, "

"It is. You sabotage every relationship right when it starts to matter. And I think it's because you're still that seven-year-old girl whose dad left, trying to make sure no one ever has that power over you again."

I wanted to argue. To explain why she was wrong. To list all the ways those men had failed me first.

But something in me knew she was right.

I'd been so busy protecting myself from the past repeating that I'd been creating the exact thing I was afraid of. My fear of abandonment was causing the abandonment.

The weight of that Tuesday morning was crushing my tomorrows.

What We Carry Without Knowing

After that conversation, I started noticing all the ways the past was running my life without my permission.

I never made long-term plans because plans could fall apart. Why get excited about something that might not happen? Why invest in a future that could be ripped away?

I kept people at arm's length even when I claimed to want connection. Getting close meant vulnerability. Vulnerability meant the potential for devastating loss.

I stayed in jobs I hated because at least they were predictable. Change might lead somewhere worse. Better the devil you know.

I hoarded money beyond any rational need for security. Because money was the one thing that couldn't leave me. Unlike people.

I never fully celebrated wins because good things didn't last. Joy was dangerous. It made you soft, unprepared for the inevitable crash.

None of this was conscious. I wasn't deliberately organizing my life around a childhood wound. But that wound was in the driver's seat anyway, making every decision, plotting every route to avoid the thing that had already happened and could never happen again because I wasn't seven anymore.

But try telling that to the seven-year-old still living in my nervous system.

The Practice of Updating the Past

My therapist Christine had me do this exercise she called "updating the timeline."

"Close your eyes," she said. "Go back to that Tuesday morning. See yourself at seven years old. What's happening?"

I went there. Saw my small self at the breakfast table. Watched my father walk out the door.

"Now," Christine said, "I want adult you to step into that scene. Go to seven-year-old you. What does she need to hear?"

I imagined myself walking over to that little girl. Kneeling down to her level.

And I told her what I wished someone had told me then: "This isn't your fault. You didn't do anything wrong. He left because of his own pain, not because of anything lacking in you. You are lovable. You are enough. And you're going to be okay. I know because I'm you, thirty years from now, and we survived this. We're okay."

I was crying now. Adult me and seven-year-old me, both crying.

"Now ask her," Christine said gently, "is she ready to let you take over? Is she ready to let adult you make the decisions instead of her?"

I asked. And in my mind's eye, that little girl nodded. Tired of being in charge. Tired of trying to protect us from something that already happened.

She handed me the reins. And something in my chest loosened.

This wasn't a one-time fix. I had to keep doing it. Keep reminding my nervous system that I'm not seven anymore. That I have resources now I didn't have then. That I can handle loss without being destroyed by it because I already have been and I'm still here.

Slowly, the grip of the past started to ease.

Why Holding Resentment Closes You to Receiving

There was a woman in my grief group named Patricia. She was seventy-three years old and had been attending the group for eleven years.

Eleven years.

She'd lost her husband thirteen years ago. And she was still, every single week, talking about how angry she was. At him for dying. At the doctors for not saving him. At God for taking him. At the universe for being cruel.

We all had compassion for her. Grief is heavy. Loss is hard. Everyone moves through it at their own pace.

But after a few months, I started noticing something: Patricia didn't want to feel better. She wanted to stay angry. The resentment had become her identity. It was how she stayed connected to her husband. It was her full-time job.

One evening, the group facilitator asked her, "Patricia, what would it mean if you let go of the anger?"

Patricia looked stricken. "I'd be betraying him. If I'm not angry about his death, it means I didn't love him enough."

"Or," the facilitator said gently, "it might mean you loved him so much that you're willing to keep living fully even though he's gone. That you're willing to receive the rest of your life as a gift instead of a punishment."

Patricia shook her head. "I can't. The anger is all I have left of him."

I watched her leave that night, hunched under the weight of her resentment, and I recognized myself in her.

Not about death. But about every hurt I was still carrying. Every person who'd wronged me. Every betrayal. Every disappointment.

I was holding onto resentment like it was precious. Like letting it go would mean those things didn't matter. Like forgiveness would let people off the hook.

But the only hook the resentment was on was mine. And it was preventing me from receiving anything new.

My Resentment Inventory

That night, I went home and made a list. Every resentment I was still carrying. Some were decades old:

My father, for leaving. (Thirty years and counting.)

My first serious boyfriend, for cheating. (Twelve years later, still bitter.)

My college roommate, for spreading rumors about me. (Ten years past, still angry when her name came up.)

My former boss, for passing me over for a promotion I deserved. (Five years gone, still fuming.)

My mother, for being critical. (A lifetime of tiny cuts that never healed.)

Myself, for every mistake, every failure, every moment I wasn't enough.

The list was long. Disturbingly long.

And as I looked at it, I realized: I was carrying all these people with me. Everywhere I went, I had an entourage of ghosts. Every person who'd ever hurt me was still living rent-free in my head, my heart, my body.

No wonder I was exhausted. No wonder I couldn't move forward. I was trying to run while carrying the dead weight of every past hurt.

What Forgiveness Actually Is

I need to be clear about something: forgiveness is not saying what they did was okay. It's not letting them off the hook. It's not reconciling or continuing the relationship.

Forgiveness is saying: "What you did hurt me. It might always hurt. But I'm not going to let that hurt run my life anymore. I'm taking my power back by putting this down."

It's for you, not for them.

I didn't need to forgive my father because he deserved it. He probably didn't. I needed to forgive him because carrying that resentment for thirty years was exhausting and it wasn't punishing him, he didn't even know I was angry. It was only punishing me.

I didn't need to forgive my ex because what he did was acceptable. It wasn't. I needed to forgive him because holding onto bitterness about a relationship that ended twelve years ago was keeping me from being fully present in new relationships.

Forgiveness is selfish. And that's exactly why it works.

The Release Ritual

I did something that felt ridiculous at the time but turned out to be transformative.

I took my resentment list to the beach. All those names, all those hurts, written on pieces of paper.

One by one, I read them out loud. Let myself feel the anger, the hurt, the betrayal. Didn't minimize it or spiritually bypass it. Just felt it fully.

Then I said: "I release you. Not because you deserve it. But because I deserve to be free."

And I burned each piece of paper in a small fire pit.

I'm not saying the burning magically healed everything. But there was something powerful about the physical act. About watching those resentments turn to ash and blow away.

When I got home, I felt lighter. Not healed completely. But lighter.

And I noticed something in the weeks that followed: when I wasn't carrying all that resentment, I had space for new things. New relationships. New opportunities. New joy.

Resentment had been taking up so much room that nothing else could fit. When I cleared it out, I could finally receive.

The Danger of Living in "Someday"

I have a friend named Lisa who's been planning to write a novel for seventeen years.

She talks about it constantly. The characters. The plot. The themes. She's done research. Created outlines. Built entire worlds in her head.

But she hasn't written a single page.

"When I have more time," she says. "When the kids are older. When I'm less busy at work. When I've taken that writing course. When I have a better setup. When I feel ready."

Someday. Always someday.

Meanwhile, seventeen years have passed. Her kids are grown. She has more free time than ever. But there's always a new reason to wait.

Because here's what I've learned about "someday": it's not a plan. It's a prison.

My Someday List

I had my own version of this. Things I was going to do... someday.

Someday, when I'm thinner, I'll go to the beach without feeling self-conscious.

Someday, when I have more money, I'll travel to Italy like I've always dreamed.

Someday, when I'm more confident, I'll put my writing out there.

Someday, when I'm healed enough, I'll be ready for a real relationship.

Someday, when I figure out my purpose, I'll start living the life I'm meant to live.

Someday. When conditions are perfect. When I'm perfect. When everything aligns just right.

Meanwhile, my life was happening now. And I was missing it. Waiting for some imaginary future where everything would be easier, better, more aligned.

The Wake-Up Call

My wake-up call came at a funeral. My grandmother's best friend, Maria, died suddenly at seventy-eight. Heart attack. No warning.

At the funeral, Maria's daughter shared stories about her mother. And one stuck with me: "Mom always said she'd take that trip to Paris someday. When she retired. When she had more time. When everything was perfect. She had the money saved. She had the time. But she never went. She died with that dream in her heart."

I looked around at the funeral. At all of us holding our someday dreams like precious things we were saving for a special occasion.

And I thought: What if there is no special occasion? What if this, right now, messy and imperfect and not-quite-ready, is all we get?

That night, I looked at my someday list and I made a decision. I was going to start doing these things now. Not when conditions were perfect. Now.

Bringing Someday Into Today

The beach thing: I went the following weekend. In my body exactly as it was. And you know what? Nobody cared what I looked like. They were too busy enjoying their own beach days.

Italy: I couldn't afford a month in Italy. But I could afford a long weekend in a small Italian town three hours away. So I went. And it was magical. Not because it was perfect or Instagram-worthy. Because I was actually doing it instead of just dreaming about it.

My writing: I started a blog. Not when I felt ready. Not when I was confident enough. Just started. Hit publish on messy, imperfect posts. And people read them. Some even said they helped.

Relationships: I stopped waiting to be healed enough and started dating as a beautifully imperfect work-in-progress. Turns out, that's what everyone else is too.

My purpose: I stopped waiting to figure it out completely and started doing what felt alive right now. And my purpose revealed itself through the doing, not through the waiting.

Each thing I moved from someday to today changed something in me. I stopped being a person who was waiting for life to start and became a person who was living life now.

How to Be Here While Moving Forward

Here's the paradox I kept running into: How do you be present in the now while also working toward a future? How do you release attachment to outcomes while still having goals? How do you stop living in "someday" without giving up on dreams?

This felt like an impossible balance. Until I learned the difference between presence and passivity.

Presence Isn't Giving Up on the Future

Being present doesn't mean you stop planning or dreaming or working toward things. It means you stop abandoning now for some imaginary perfect later.

I learned this from my ceramics teacher, Diane, who I keep coming back to because she understood this better than anyone.

One day I asked her, "How do you stay present while you're creating something? Aren't you always thinking about the finished piece?"

She laughed. "If I spend the whole time thinking about the finished piece, I ruin the piece I'm making. I need to be here, with this clay, in this moment, making this choice. The finished piece emerges from a thousand present moments, not from obsessing about the outcome."

"But you must have some vision of what you're making?"

"Of course. I have intention. Direction. But I hold it lightly. I'm more interested in this moment of creation than in whether it matches my vision. Sometimes the clay wants to be something different than what I planned. And that's usually better."

This is the balance: hold intention without strangling it with attachment. Move toward the future while being fully here now.

The Practice of Present-Forward Living

I developed what I call "present-forward living", a way of being that honors both presence and direction.

Every morning, I ask two questions:

1. What wants to happen today? (Present)
2. What small step moves me toward what matters? (Forward)

Not "What should I do to achieve my goals?" That's future-focused and creates anxiety.

Not "What do I feel like doing?" That can be present but directionless.

Both questions together create movement that's grounded in now.

I plan, but I hold plans lightly.

I have goals. I make plans. But I'm willing to revise them based on what's actually happening instead of forcing reality to match my blueprint.

Plans are guides, not mandates.

I celebrate the process, not just outcomes.

Instead of waiting to celebrate when I achieve the thing, I celebrate the small moments along the way. The good conversation. The hard choice. The tiny step forward.

This keeps me from living entirely in the future, waiting for the big win that will finally make me happy.

I practice being exactly where I am.

Even when where I am isn't where I want to be. Even when I'm working toward something else.

I can be in a job I'm planning to leave while still being present with my colleagues.

I can be single and dating while still enjoying my life alone.

I can be working toward financial goals while appreciating what I have now.

This isn't settling. It's refusing to abandon the present moment while reaching for the future.

The Both/And Practice

The biggest shift came when I stopped thinking in either/or and started thinking in both/and.

Not: "Either I accept where I am OR I work toward something better."
But: "I can accept where I am AND work toward something better."

Not: "Either I let go of the past OR I honor its impact on me."
But: "I can release the grip of the past AND acknowledge how it shaped me."

Not: "Either I'm present in now OR I plan for the future."
But: "I can be fully here AND move intentionally forward."

Both/and thinking creates space for complexity. For nuance. For the full human experience of being here while also becoming.

REFLECTION: Your Timeline Inventory

Take some time with these questions. Don't rush. Let the answers emerge honestly.

The Past:

What are you still carrying from yesterday? Which resentments are you holding? Which hurts are still running your decisions?

Write them down. See them clearly. Then ask: What would it cost to keep carrying this? What might become possible if I put it down?

The Future:

What's on your "someday" list? What are you waiting for perfect conditions to do?

Choose one thing. Just one. How could you bring a version of it into today? Not perfectly. Not completely. Just somehow.

The Present:

Where are you right now, in this moment, that you're not fully inhabiting because you're stuck in past or future?

What's here, right now, that's good enough to appreciate even while you work toward more?

This isn't about fixing anything. It's about seeing clearly. Because you can't release what you can't see.

And what you can see, you can choose to put down.

The past already happened. The future hasn't arrived. This moment, right now, reading these words, this is where your life is actually happening.

Don't miss it by living anywhere else.

PART NINE: THE DAILY PRACTICE

Living the Undo Principle

Morning: Starting From Allowing Instead of Forcing

For three years, I had the same morning routine. It started at 5:00 AM with my alarm blaring some motivational podcast about crushing your goals and dominating your day.

I'd force myself out of bed, even when my body was begging for more sleep, because "successful people wake up early."

Meditate for twenty minutes. Not because I wanted to, but because it was on the routine.

Visualize my perfect day. Journal three pages of affirmations. Review my vision board. Do a gratitude practice. Green smoothie. Workout. Shower with specific intentions. Get dressed in clothes that made me "feel abundant."

By 7:30 AM, I'd completed seventeen separate tasks designed to "set my vibration high" for the day.

I was also exhausted, resentful, and already behind schedule.

This routine was supposed to make me feel empowered and aligned. Instead, it made me feel like I was failing before the day even started. Because if I missed even one step, if I slept through the alarm or didn't have time for the full workout or couldn't get through all three journal pages, I'd spend the whole day anxious that I'd ruined my manifestation potential.

The morning routine wasn't serving me. I was serving it. And I was so busy performing my perfectly optimized morning that I wasn't actually present for my life.

The Morning Everything Changed

It was a Saturday. My alarm went off at 5:00 AM like always. I reached over to turn it off and just... didn't get up.

Not in a defiant way. Not even a conscious decision. My body just said "no" and I listened.

I slept until 8:30. Woke up naturally, without an alarm. And for the first few seconds, before my mind kicked in, I felt peaceful.

Then the panic started. "You overslept. You missed your routine. You didn't set your vibration. The whole day is already ruined. You're so undisciplined. Successful people don't sleep until 8:30."

But instead of jumping into damage control mode, I just lay there and asked myself a question I'd never asked before: What if there's nothing to fix?

What if I could just... start the day from here? From this moment? Without needing to compensate for the "wrong" start?

I got up slowly. Made coffee without any specific intention except enjoying coffee. Sat on my balcony and watched the morning light without journaling about it or posting it or making it mean something about my spiritual growth.

I didn't meditate. Didn't visualize. Didn't review my vision board. Just drank coffee and existed.

And the day didn't fall apart. In fact, it was one of the best days I'd had in months. Because I started from allowing instead of forcing.

What "Allowing" Actually Looks Like

After that Saturday, I redesigned my entire relationship with mornings. Not by creating a new, better routine. By releasing the idea that I needed a routine at all.

Now my mornings look different every day. Because I'm responding to what's actually here instead of forcing myself through a predetermined sequence.

Some mornings, I wake up early naturally. Not because I should, but because my body is done sleeping. On those days, I enjoy the quiet. Maybe I journal. Maybe I just sit. Maybe I go for a walk. Whatever feels alive.

Some mornings, I sleep until 9:00. Because my body needed rest. And instead of berating myself, I thank my body for telling me what it needs and me for finally listening.

Some mornings, I want to meditate. So I do. Not for a specific amount of time or with a specific technique. Just sitting with breath until it feels complete.

Some mornings, I don't want to meditate. So I don't. And nothing terrible happens.

Some mornings, I wake up anxious or sad or uncomfortable. And instead of immediately trying to fix it or shift it or transmute it into something more acceptable, I just acknowledge it. "Good morning, anxiety. I see you're here today."

The practice isn't about doing the right things in the right order. It's about meeting myself where I actually am instead of where I think I should be.

The Five-Minute Morning Practice

I did create one simple practice that helps me start from allowing. It takes about five minutes, and it's the only non-negotiable part of my morning.

Minute 1: Check In
Before I do anything, before I look at my phone, before I get out of bed, before I start planning the day, I check in with my body.

How do I feel right now? Not how should I feel. How do I actually feel?

Tired? Rested? Anxious? Peaceful? Heavy? Light? Excited? Resistant?

Just notice. No judgment. Just data.

Minute 2: Ask What's Needed
Based on how I actually feel, what does this body-mind-heart system need today?

Not what should it need. Not what would make me more productive or high-vibe or successful.

What does it actually need?

Sometimes the answer is movement. Sometimes rest. Sometimes connection. Sometimes solitude. Sometimes gentle structure. Sometimes complete spaciousness.

Minute 3: Set One Intention
Not seventeen intentions. Not a whole list of affirmations. One simple intention for how I want to move through today.

Not "I will be abundant and successful and high-vibe."

More like: "I will notice when I'm forcing and practice allowing instead."
Or: "I will choose ease over effort when possible."
Or: "I will be kind to myself when I mess up."
Or simply: "I will pay attention."

Minutes 4-5: Three Breaths
Three slow, conscious breaths. That's it. Not a whole meditation. Just three breaths to arrive in my body, in this day, in this moment.

That's the practice. Five minutes. But those five minutes set a completely different tone than my old two-hour routine did.

Because I'm starting from where I am, not from where I think I should be.

Throughout the Day: Noticing Gripping vs. Flowing

About six months into my release practice, I was having lunch with my friend Maya when she suddenly stopped mid-sentence and stared at me.

"What?" I asked.

"You just did it," she said.

"Did what?"

"That thing you do. Your shoulders just crept up to your ears. Your jaw got tight. Your whole body just contracted."

I hadn't even noticed. But she was right. I'd been talking about a work situation and my body had gone into full grip mode without my conscious awareness.

"How often do you think you do that?" she asked.

I started paying attention. The answer was horrifying: constantly.

The Grip I Couldn't See

Once I started noticing, I saw the gripping everywhere:

Physical gripping: Shoulders up by my ears. Jaw clenched. Holding my breath. Hands in fists. Stomach tight. Chest constricted.

Mental gripping: Obsessively planning. Replaying conversations. Trying to control outcomes. Spinning in worst-case scenarios. Can't let a thought go.

Emotional gripping: Holding onto irritation from three hours ago. Clutching anxiety instead of letting it move through. Refusing to let joy be just joy because what if it doesn't last?

Relational gripping: Monitoring someone's mood to see if they're mad at me. Trying to control how people see me. Needing specific responses. Can't let a conversation end naturally.

I was gripping my way through life, and I'd been doing it for so long I didn't even know what flowing felt like anymore.

The Body as Early Warning System

I learned that my body always knows I'm gripping before my mind does. My nervous system registers the clutching and contracts in response. But I'd been so disconnected from my body that I was missing all the signals.

So I started developing what I call "grip awareness", paying attention to the physical sensations that tell me I've shifted from flow to force.

Breathing: When I'm flowing, my breath is natural, easy, reaching my belly. When I'm gripping, my breath gets shallow, stuck in my chest, or I'm holding it altogether.

Jaw: Flow = relaxed. Gripping = clenched so tight it gives me headaches.

Shoulders: Flow = settled, dropped. Gripping = creeping up toward my ears like they're trying to become earrings.

Stomach: Flow = soft, relaxed. Gripping = tight knot of tension.

Hands: Flow = loose, open. Gripping = literally making fists or tensing.

Pace: Flow = moving at a sustainable rhythm. Gripping = rushing, frantic, can't slow down.

Now I check in with these indicators throughout the day. Not obsessively. Just periodically: What's my body doing right now?

And when I notice gripping, I don't judge it. I just notice and ask: What am I trying to control right now?

The Micro-Release Practice

Once I notice I'm gripping, I do what I call a "micro-release." It takes about thirty seconds.

Step 1: Name it.
"I'm gripping right now. I'm trying to control [whatever it is]."

Just naming it loosens the grip slightly. Bringing it into consciousness gives me choice.

Step 2: Feel where it lives.
Where is this grip in my body? Shoulders? Jaw? Stomach?

I put my attention there. Not to fix it, just to acknowledge it.

Step 3: One conscious release.
Usually, this is a deep exhale. Sometimes it's dropping my shoulders. Sometimes it's unclenching my jaw. Sometimes it's opening my hands.

Whatever feels like the opposite of the gripping.

Step 4: Ask one question.
"What if I didn't have to control this?"

I don't need to answer it. Just asking it creates a small opening. A possibility that I could let go.

That's it. Thirty seconds. But doing this five, ten, fifteen times throughout the day completely changes how I move through my life.

Real Examples from Real Days

Example 1: The Morning Email

I open my laptop and see an email from my boss requesting a meeting. No context. Just "Can we talk this afternoon?"

My body immediately grips. Stomach knots. Breath shallow. Mind spinning: "What did I do wrong? Am I in trouble? Is this about that project? Should I prepare a defense?"

I notice the grip. Name it: "I'm trying to control what this meeting is about and what my boss thinks of me."

I feel it in my stomach. Take a breath. Drop my shoulders.

Ask: "What if I didn't have to control this?"

The grip doesn't disappear completely, but it loosens enough that I can respond with "Sure, 2pm works" instead of spending three hours catastrophizing.

Example 2: The Social Situation

I'm at a party. Someone I want to impress is talking to someone else. My whole body contracts. I start performing, laugh louder, talk more animatedly, position myself where they'll notice me.

I catch myself. Notice the grip: "I'm trying to control whether this person likes me."

Feel it in my chest, tight, performing, not breathing naturally.

Release: One big exhale. Let my shoulders drop. Stop performing.

Ask: "What if I didn't have to control whether they like me?"

Suddenly I can just be at the party instead of managing everyone's perception of me.

Example 3: The Difficult Conversation

I need to have a hard conversation with a friend. All day, I'm rehearsing what I'll say, anticipating her responses, planning my rebuttals.

My jaw is so tight it hurts.

I notice. Name it: "I'm trying to control how this conversation goes."

Feel it in my jaw. Take a breath. Let my jaw relax.

Ask: "What if I didn't have to control how this goes?"

The preparation was making me more anxious, not less. When I release the need to control the conversation, I can just show up honestly and respond to what actually happens instead of the seventeen scenarios I made up.

Evening: The Release Ritual That Resets Everything

By the time I get to evening, I've accumulated a day's worth of gripping. Even with micro-releases throughout the day, there's residue. Tension I didn't fully release. Concerns I'm still holding. Energy that needs to be discharged.

For years, my evening routine was just like my morning one: a long list of things I "should" do to process the day properly. Gratitude journaling. Reviewing my wins. Planning tomorrow. More affirmations. More visualizing.

It was exhausting. And it kept me in my head instead of helping me land in my body.

Now I have what I call the "Evening Release Ritual." It's simple, physical, and actually works.

The Ritual (15-20 minutes)

Part 1: The Physical Download (5 minutes)

I do something physical to help my body discharge the accumulated tension of the day. Different things work on different days:

Some days it's shaking. Literally shaking my body, arms, legs, torso, like a dog shaking off water. It looks ridiculous. It feels amazing. All that held energy moves.

Some days it's stretching. Not yoga with proper form. Just moving my body in whatever ways feel good, making whatever sounds want to come out.

Some days it's dancing. Putting on music and moving without caring how it looks.

Some days it's just lying on the floor and letting my body be heavy, supported by the ground.

The point isn't to do it right. It's to help my nervous system complete the stress cycles that got started during the day but never finished.

Part 2: The Mind Release (5 minutes)

I write down everything I'm still holding onto from the day. Not in a journal. On scratch paper that I'm going to throw away.

All the worries, resentments, things I said wrong, things I should have done differently, conversations I'm still replaying, concerns about tomorrow.

Stream of consciousness. No editing. No making it coherent.

Just dump it all out of my head onto paper.

Then I literally throw it away. Sometimes I tear it up first. Sometimes I burn it if I'm feeling dramatic. Usually I just crumple it up and toss it.

The physical act of throwing it away helps my brain register: we're done with this now. We're putting it down.

Part 3: The Gratitude That's Actually Honest (3-5 minutes)

I'm not against gratitude practice. I'm against forced gratitude practice where you're supposed to be grateful for everything all the time even when things are hard.

So I do honest gratitude. I notice three things from the day that were actually good. Not the things I think I should be grateful for. Things that genuinely felt good.

Sometimes it's big: "That conversation with my friend was so connecting and real."

Sometimes it's tiny: "My coffee was perfect this morning."

Sometimes it's weird: "I'm grateful I didn't punch that person who was rude to me in line."

Real gratitude. For what was actually good, not what I'm supposed to appreciate.

Part 4: The Set-Down (2-3 minutes)

I physically set down anything I'm still carrying from the day.

Sometimes I visualize it: Okay, I'm putting down this worry about the work thing. I'm putting down this anxiety about that conversation. I'm putting down my need to figure out that problem tonight.

Sometimes I actually use objects: I'll pick up a stone or a book or whatever's nearby and imagine transferring the concern into it, then setting it on a shelf. "I'm putting this here for tonight. If it's still important tomorrow, I can pick it up again."

The point is to practice the physical sensation of putting things down. Of not carrying everything into sleep with me.

Part 5: The Tomorrow Intention (1 minute)

Not a whole plan. Not a list of goals. Just one simple intention for tomorrow.

"Tomorrow, I will move a little slower."
"Tomorrow, I will notice beauty."
"Tomorrow, I will be kind to myself when things are hard."

Something simple that helps me land in the next day with some gentle direction.

What This Ritual Actually Does

This evening practice does something my old routine never did: it helps me actually transition out of the day.

Before, I'd just carry everything into sleep with me. I'd lie in bed replaying the day, planning tomorrow, worrying about seventeen different things.

Now, I sleep better. Because I've completed the day. Released what needs releasing. Set down what I can't solve tonight.

And I wake up with less accumulated tension. Because I'm not starting each day carrying yesterday and the day before and the day before that.

It's like emptying a backpack every night instead of adding more rocks to it daily until you can barely move.

Knowing When to Act and When to Wait

This is the question I get asked most: "How do you know when to take action versus when to wait? How do you tell the difference between trusting the process and just being passive?"

It's a good question. Because letting go doesn't mean doing nothing. And trusting doesn't mean being passive.

But I spent years getting this wrong. Acting from anxiety and calling it ambition. Waiting from fear and calling it trust.

I had to learn to tell the difference.

The Two Types of Action

There are really only two types of action: forced and inspired.

Forced action comes from anxiety, desperation, or should. It feels like pushing. Like you have to make something happen or something bad will occur.

Inspired action comes from genuine pull, from aliveness, from desire that's not desperate. It feels like responding. Like moving toward something because it's calling you.

The challenge is that they can look identical from the outside. Someone watching me wouldn't necessarily be able to tell if I was taking a job because I was desperate and terrified of running out of money, or because I was genuinely excited about the opportunity.

But I can feel the difference in my body.

The Body Test

I learned to check in with my body before taking action. Because my body always knows the difference between forced and inspired, even when my mind is confused.

Forced action feels like:

- Contraction in my chest or stomach
- Shallow breathing
- A sense of urgency that borders on panic
- "I have to do this or else"
- Depletion, even thinking about it makes me tired
- No joy in it, just pressure

Inspired action feels like:

- Expansion in my chest
- Full, easy breathing
- Excitement that might include nervousness but isn't pure anxiety
- "I want to do this" or "Something in me is saying yes"
- Energy, thinking about it gives me energy
- There's aliveness in it, even if it's scary

I started using this as my litmus test. Before saying yes to anything, before making any significant decision, I'd pause and check: Does this feel like force or inspiration?

Real Examples

Example 1: The Job Offer

I got two job offers at the same time. On paper, Job A was clearly better, higher pay, better title, more prestigious company.

But when I sat with it and checked in with my body, I felt contraction. The thought of accepting made my stomach tight. I'd be taking it because I "should", because it looked good, because it was the smart move financially, because people would be impressed.

Job B paid less. Wasn't as impressive on LinkedIn. But when I thought about it, I felt expansion. Genuine excitement. My breath deepened instead of shallowing.

I took Job B. Best decision I ever made. Not because it led to some amazing outcome, though it did, but because I was moving from inspiration instead of force.

Example 2: The Relationship Decision

I was dating someone who was nice enough, interested enough, checked enough boxes. But something felt off.

My friends said, "Give it more time. Maybe you're just scared of commitment."

So I checked in with my body. When I imagined continuing the relationship, I felt heavy. Obligated. Like I was doing it because I should give nice people a chance, not because I was genuinely drawn to him.

When I imagined ending it, I felt guilty, but also light. Free. Like I could breathe again.

I ended it. Even though there was nothing "wrong" with him. Because my body was clearly saying "this isn't it" and I was finally listening.

Example 3: The Project Proposal

A colleague approached me about collaborating on a project. It aligned with my goals. It would be good for my career. It made strategic sense.

But I felt nothing. No excitement. No pull. Just a sense of "this would be the smart thing to do."

I almost said yes anyway. Because it made sense. Because I should be more strategic. Because you're supposed to say yes to good opportunities.

But I checked in first. And my body was clear: no aliveness here. This is force, not inspiration.

I declined. And two weeks later, an opportunity came up that I was genuinely excited about. If I'd said yes to the first one, I wouldn't have had space for the second.

When to Wait

Knowing when to wait is harder than knowing when to act. Because waiting can feel like doing nothing. Like being passive. Like missing opportunities.

But sometimes waiting is the most powerful action you can take.

Wait when:

- Every option feels forced, and nothing feels inspired
- You're in crisis mode and every "solution" is just panic
- Something says "not yet" and you can't articulate why
- You're being pushed by external pressure but have no internal yes
- You're exhausted and running on fumes, rest first, then decide

The test: If you're waiting from trust (I'm allowing the right timing to emerge), your body feels settled. If you're waiting from fear (I'm too scared to move), your body feels frozen.

Trust-waiting has peace in it, even if there's also uncertainty. Fear-waiting has contraction in it.

PRACTICE: Your Daily Check-Ins

This week, try building these simple check-ins into your day:

Morning: Before you do anything, ask: How do I actually feel? What does this body-mind-heart need today? Set one simple intention.

Throughout the day: Set three alarms on your phone labeled "GRIP CHECK." When they go off, notice: Where am I gripping right now? Can I release it, even slightly?

Evening: Spend 15 minutes doing some version of the release ritual. Move your body. Dump your thoughts. Notice real gratitude. Set something down.

Before decisions: Check in with your body. Does this feel like force or inspiration? Wait for the answer.

These aren't rigid rules. They're invitations to pay attention. To notice when you're gripping versus flowing. To start from where you are instead of where you think you should be.

The practice isn't about doing it perfectly. It's about doing it at all.

One check-in. One release. One moment of noticing.

That's how you live the undo principle: not through one big transformation, but through a thousand small moments of letting go.

PART TEN: LIFE AFTER LETTING GO

Integration and Transformation

What Actually Changes When You Finally Release

I wish I could tell you there was one dramatic moment when everything shifted. A lightning bolt of enlightenment. A day I woke up completely transformed, all my old patterns dissolved, living in perfect flow forever.

That's not what happened.

What happened was quieter. Slower. More like the way spring arrives, not all at once, but in a series of small thaws until one day you realize the entire landscape has changed.

About eight months into my release practice, I was having coffee with my friend Rachel. We were talking about nothing important, her terrible date, my annoying neighbor, the weird weather we'd been having.

She stopped mid-sentence and just looked at me.

"What?" I asked.

"You're different," she said.

"Different how?"

"I don't know exactly. But something fundamental has shifted. You seem... lighter? More here? I can't put my finger on it, but you're not the same person you were a year ago."

I thought about it. She was right. I was different. But the changes were so gradual I hadn't noticed them accumulating.

The Changes Nobody Tells You About

Here's what actually changed, not the dramatic before-and-after story, but the real, lived experience of what releasing does over time:

I stopped performing my life and started living it.

I used to curate everything. Every social media post was calculated to create a certain impression. Every conversation was monitored, am I being interesting enough? Funny enough? Spiritual enough?

Now I just... am. I post things because I want to, not because I'm managing my image. I have conversations because I'm actually interested, not because I'm networking or performing.

The constant exhaustion of maintaining a persona? Gone. And I didn't even realize how heavy it was until I put it down.

My relationships got simpler and deeper.

I lost some friends when I stopped being who they needed me to be. The ones who wanted me to be the always-positive cheerleader. The ones who bonded with me over complaining. The ones who liked the performing version better than the real one.

That hurt. But the relationships that remained got so much richer. Because I stopped trying to control how people saw me, they could actually see me. And the people who stayed? They're the ones who wanted the real thing.

I became boring in the best way.

My life used to be full of drama. Constant crisis. Always something urgent happening. And I thought that meant I was living fully, intensely, passionately.

Turns out I was just in constant sympathetic nervous system activation. Addicted to the adrenaline of chaos because calm felt like death.

Now my life is quieter. More predictable. I have routines that I actually enjoy instead of routines I force myself through. I have boring Saturdays where I just read and putter around my apartment.

It's not Instagram-worthy. It's also the most peaceful I've ever been.

Small things stopped being catastrophes.

I used to have a breakdown if I spilled coffee on my shirt. If someone didn't text back. If plans changed. Everything felt like evidence that I was doing life wrong.

Now when I spill coffee, I just clean it up. When someone doesn't text back, I assume they're busy. When plans change, I adapt.

I don't know when this shift happened. But somewhere along the way, I stopped treating every minor inconvenience like a personal attack from the universe.

I started trusting myself.

This is the big one. For years, I second-guessed every decision. Consulted everyone. Pulled tarot cards. Looked for signs. Needed external validation before I could move.

Now I just... know what I want. And I trust that knowing. I still mess up sometimes. Make wrong calls. Take paths that don't work out.

But I trust myself to handle it. To adjust. To figure it out.

That trust, that unshakeable sense that I can handle whatever comes, that's the real transformation.

What Didn't Change (And That's Okay)

I also need to be honest about what didn't change. Because the manifestation world sells this idea that once you "do the work," everything becomes perfect and easy and aligned.

That's bullshit.

I still have hard days. Days where everything feels difficult. Where I'm tired or sad or anxious for no clear reason. Letting go didn't make me immune to being human.

I still have challenges. Money is still sometimes tight. Relationships still take work. My body still has issues. Life didn't become a highlight reel.

I still grip sometimes. I still catch myself trying to control outcomes, forcing timelines, clutching at certainty. The old patterns haven't completely disappeared.

I still don't have all the answers. I don't know my life purpose with crystal clarity. I don't have everything figured out. I'm still navigating uncertainty.

The difference is that none of this means I'm doing it wrong anymore. Hard days are just hard days. Challenges are just life. Gripping is just a pattern I notice and release. Uncertainty is just the price of being alive.

I'm not trying to transcend the human experience anymore. I'm just trying to have it more honestly.

The Unexpected Gifts That Show Up

About a year into my practice, gifts started appearing that I never manifested, never visualized, never put on a vision board. They just... showed up. Because I'd finally created space for them.

Gift One: Synchronicity That Wasn't Forced

I used to see synchronicities everywhere because I was desperately looking for them. Every number sequence was a sign. Every song on the radio was a message. Every "coincidence" meant something about my manifestation.

I was manufacturing meaning to reassure myself I was on the right path.

Now I don't look for signs. But they show up anyway. Real ones. The kind that make you go "huh, that's weird" instead of "OMG THE UNIVERSE IS SPEAKING TO ME."

Like the time I was thinking about my grandmother and someone in line at the coffee shop was wearing her signature perfume. I hadn't smelled it in years. It stopped me cold. Made me cry right there in public.

Or the time I randomly picked up a book at a used bookstore and it had a note in the margin that answered a question I'd been sitting with for weeks.

These moments feel different than the signs I used to force. They're gentler. Quieter. Like life is winking at me instead of screaming instructions.

Gift Two: Creativity I Didn't Know I Had

For years, I wanted to write. But I was so busy trying to manifest being a writer that I never actually wrote.

I was too focused on the outcome. On whether it was good enough. On what it would mean about me if I succeeded or failed.

Once I let go of needing writing to be anything, not a career, not proof of my worth, not evidence that I was creative, I just started writing. For myself. Because I wanted to.

No pressure. No vision board. Just putting words on a page because it felt good.

And something opened up. Ideas came. Stories emerged. A voice I didn't know I had started speaking.

I'm not a famous author. I don't make my living from writing. But I write now. Regularly. Joyfully. And that feels like a bigger gift than any external success.

The release of outcome created space for the actual thing.

Gift Three: The Right People at the Right Time

When I was desperately manifesting relationships, friendships, romance, business connections, I attracted desperate people. Or people who liked the performed version of me. Or people I tried to force into roles they didn't actually fit.

When I stopped trying to attract anyone and just focused on being myself, different people started showing up.

My current partner, Marcus, is someone I never would have manifested. He doesn't match my old list. He doesn't fit the vision board version of my ideal relationship.

But he's so much better than what I thought I wanted. Because he loves the real me, not the curated version. Because our relationship is built on actual compatibility instead of desperate need. Because I didn't have to force or chase or convince.

He just... appeared. When I'd stopped looking. When I was genuinely content being alone.

Same with friends. Same with work connections. The right people showed up when I stopped trying to collect them.

Gift Four: Peace That Isn't Dependent on Circumstances

This is the gift I didn't even know was possible.

I used to think peace came from having everything figured out. From achieving my goals. From finally being successful enough, healed enough, manifested enough.

But that kind of peace was always conditional. Always dependent on external circumstances staying favorable.

This new peace is different. It's not dependent on everything going well. It's not shattered by difficulty or uncertainty or things not working out.

It's a baseline settling in my nervous system. A quiet knowing that I'm okay even when things aren't okay.

I can have a terrible day and still have peace underneath it. I can face challenges and still feel fundamentally settled.

It's not the absence of difficulty. It's the presence of trust. Trust that I can handle this. Trust that it's all part of the process. Trust that I don't need to control everything to be safe.

This peace? This is the real manifestation. And it came not from getting what I wanted, but from releasing my grip on needing anything to be different than it is.

Gift Five: The Ability to Enjoy "Not Yet"

I spent decades living in "not yet." Not yet successful. Not yet healed. Not yet where I wanted to be. And "not yet" felt like failure. Like a problem to solve. Like evidence that I wasn't manifesting correctly.

Now "not yet" feels like possibility. Like being in process. Like the interesting part of the story.

I have goals. Things I'm working toward. But I don't need to be there already to be okay here.

I can enjoy where I am while moving toward where I'm going. The journey isn't just something to endure until I reach the destination. It's the actual thing.

This shift, from "not yet" as failure to "not yet" as alive possibility, might be the biggest gift of all.

When the Grip Returns: Coming Back Without Shame

Here's what nobody tells you about transformation: it's not linear. You don't just release the grip once and live in flow forever.

The grip comes back. Over and over. Sometimes for minutes. Sometimes for days. Sometimes you find yourself right back in old patterns you thought you'd released months ago.

And when it happens, when you notice you've been white-knuckling your way through the last week, when you catch yourself forcing and controlling and desperately manifesting again, the temptation is to shame yourself.

"I thought I was past this. I should know better by now. Why am I still doing this? All that work and I'm right back where I started."

I've had to learn that the grip returning isn't failure. It's just being human. And how I meet it makes all the difference.

The Day I Found Myself Gripping Again

About eighteen months into my release practice, I had what I can only describe as a full regression.

I was going through a stressful work situation. A project I cared about was falling apart. And slowly, so slowly I didn't notice it happening, I started gripping again.

Checking my email obsessively. Trying to control outcomes. Planning seventeen different scenarios. Losing sleep. Getting anxious and tight and desperate.

One morning, I woke up and realized: I'm doing it again. All of it. The forcing, the controlling, the death-grip on outcomes. I'm right back in the beautiful prison I thought I'd left.

My first reaction was shame. Disappointment in myself. "After all this work, I'm still the same. I haven't changed at all. What was the point?"

But then I remembered something my therapist Christine had told me: "You're not back at the beginning. You're in a spiral. You pass through the same issues, but each time at a higher level. Each time with more awareness."

And she was right. Because even though I was gripping, I could see that I was gripping. I could name it. Feel it in my body. Recognize the pattern.

The old me would have gripped for months without even noticing. Without seeing it as a choice. Without having any tools to shift.

The new me noticed within a week. And had a choice about what to do next.

The Practice of Coming Back

I've developed a practice for when I notice the grip has returned. Not a way to shame myself back into alignment, but a compassionate way to come back to release.

Step 1: Notice Without Judgment

"Oh. I'm gripping again. Interesting."

Not "I'm failing again." Not "I should be past this." Just neutral observation: the grip is here.

Step 2: Get Curious

"What's underneath this grip? What am I afraid of?"

Usually, there's a fear driving the control. Fear of failure. Fear of loss. Fear of being hurt. When I can see the fear, I can have compassion for the gripping instead of shame.

Step 3: Acknowledge What's Real

"This situation is hard. It makes sense that I'm trying to control it. Of course I'm scared. Of course I want to force an outcome. That's human."

Validating the grip instead of fighting it actually makes it easier to release.

Step 4: One Small Release

Not trying to let go of everything at once. Just: What's one small thing I could put down right now?

Maybe it's releasing control of one small aspect of the situation. Maybe it's just taking one full breath. Maybe it's just unclenching my jaw.

One small release. That's enough.

Step 5: Remember What I Know

I've done this before. I've let go before. I know how.

Not as pressure ("I should be able to do this"), but as evidence ("I have these tools. I can use them").

This practice has saved me countless times. Because it allows the grip to return without that return meaning I've failed or lost all my progress.

The Spiral, Not the Circle

Christine's image of the spiral stuck with me. Because it's true: you do encounter the same issues again. The same fears. The same patterns. The same tendencies to grip.

But you're not in the same place you were before.

The first time through: I gripped unconsciously. Didn't even know I was doing it. Stayed there for years.

The second time through: I gripped for months before noticing. But I did eventually notice. And I had some tools to shift.

The third time through: I gripped for weeks. Noticed faster. Released easier.

The fourth time through: I gripped for days. Saw it quickly. Knew exactly what to do.

The fifth time through: I gripped for hours. Caught it almost immediately. Released almost as fast.

Each time, the pattern is the same but my relationship to it is different. I'm moving through it faster. With more awareness. With more compassion for myself.

That's the spiral. You're not going in circles. You're going up, even when it feels like you're covering the same ground.

Permission to Be Human

The most important thing I've learned about the grip returning: it doesn't mean you're doing it wrong.

You're not supposed to transcend being human. You're not supposed to reach some elevated state where you never struggle or grip or fall back into old patterns.

You're supposed to be human. Which means sometimes you grip. And that's okay.

The practice isn't achieving perfect release. It's noticing when you're gripping and choosing, when you're ready, to let go again.

And again. And again. For the rest of your life.

That's not failure. That's the practice.

How Your Freedom Becomes Medicine for Others

I didn't set out to teach anyone about letting go. I was just trying to figure out my own life. To stop suffocating under my own grip. To find some peace.

But something strange started happening once I changed.

People noticed.

The Conversations That Started

It began with small comments.

"You seem different. More relaxed. What changed?"

"I don't know how to explain it, but you feel more... real now?"

"You're not as stressed as you used to be. What are you doing?"

At first, I'd deflect. "Oh, I'm just working on some stuff." Because I didn't want to become one of those people who'd found something and now had to evangelize about it.

But people kept asking. And eventually, I started sharing. Not as advice. Just as my experience.

"I stopped trying to control everything. I'm practicing letting go."

And the responses were striking. Not "that sounds weird" or "how new age." More like: "Oh my god, can you tell me more?"

People were hungry for this. Starving for permission to stop trying so hard. Desperate for someone to tell them it was okay to release the grip.

The Friend Who Called at Midnight

The first time my freedom became medicine for someone else, it was my friend Jessica. The one I'd grown apart from when I stopped being available for our complaint sessions.

She called me at midnight, crying. "I can't do this anymore. I can't keep trying so hard and failing and trying harder. I'm so tired, Sofia. I don't know what to do."

I could have given her advice. Told her what to do. Fixed it for her.

Instead, I just told her the truth: "You don't have to do anything. You don't have to try harder. You don't have to fix this tonight. You just have to be here, right now, crying on the phone with me. That's enough."

She was quiet for a long time. Then: "I don't think anyone has ever told me I don't have to do anything."

We talked for an hour. I didn't give her a step-by-step plan. Didn't tell her how to manifest her way out. Just shared what I'd learned: that sometimes the most powerful thing you can do is stop doing and start allowing.

Six months later, she called again. "I wanted to tell you something. That conversation changed my life. I started practicing what you said, just being instead of constantly doing. And everything is different now. Not perfect, but different. Lighter. I can breathe."

That's when I understood: my freedom was contagious.

What Permission Actually Looks Like

You don't have to become a teacher or a coach or write a book to let your freedom be medicine for others.

You just have to live it. And give people permission through your example.

Permission to be imperfect. When people see you being honest about your struggles instead of performing perfection, it gives them permission to stop performing too.

Permission to rest. When people see you saying no to things, prioritizing sleep, taking breaks, they start to wonder if they could do that too.

Permission to quit. When people see you leaving something that isn't working, a job, a relationship, a path, it shows them that quitting isn't always giving up. Sometimes it's choosing yourself.

Permission to not know. When people see you comfortable with uncertainty instead of desperately grasping for answers, it gives them permission to sit in their own not-knowing.

Permission to be human. When people see you having hard days and bad moments and still being fundamentally okay, it shows them that they don't have to be spiritually advanced or always high-vibe or perfectly healed.

You give all this permission not through preaching, but through living. Through being the example of what's possible when you stop trying so hard.

The Ripple Effect I Didn't Expect

Two years into my release practice, I ran into my old boss. The one from the toxic job I'd quit.

We grabbed coffee to catch up. She was asking about my life now, and I was honest: "It's quieter. Less impressive on paper. But I'm happy. Actually happy, not performing happiness."

She got quiet. Then: "Can I tell you something? Watching you quit changed something for me. You were the golden employee. If anyone was going to stay and make it work, it was you. When you left, I realized: if Sofia can walk away from this, maybe it really is toxic. Maybe it's not just me being weak."

She paused. "I quit three months after you did. Best decision I ever made. But I don't know if I would have had the courage without seeing you do it first."

I had no idea she'd been watching. No idea that my choice to leave would give her permission to leave too.

That's how freedom spreads. Not through convincing people. Through living differently and letting that difference speak for itself.

You Don't Have to Save Anyone

Here's the important part: your freedom is medicine, but you're not responsible for healing anyone.

You're not here to save people. You're not here to convince anyone to let go. You're not here to make people change.

You're just here to live your own life with more freedom, more ease, more authenticity.

Some people will notice. Some will ask questions. Some will be inspired to try it themselves.

Some won't. And that's okay too.

Your job is just to keep releasing your own grip. To keep choosing ease over force. To keep being real instead of performing.

The medicine isn't in what you say or teach. It's in how you live.

And people who are ready? They'll feel it. They'll ask. They'll learn.

Not because you convinced them. But because your freedom gave them permission to imagine their own.

REFLECTION: Your Own After

Before you close this chapter, take a moment to notice:

What's different now than when you started this book?

Maybe nothing major. Maybe just small shifts. But notice them. Name them. Let yourself see the changes, even the tiny ones.

What unexpected gifts have shown up?

Not the things you manifested or worked for. The things that just appeared when you created space.

When has your grip returned?

And how did you come back? What did you learn about yourself in the returning?

Who has noticed your shift?

Even if no one has said anything directly, who seems to respond to you differently now?

You don't have to have dramatic answers. This isn't about measuring transformation against some standard.

It's just about noticing: something is different. Something has shifted.

And that shift, however small, is real. It's yours. It's enough.

You've started to live differently. And that difference is already medicine, even if you can't see all the ways it's spreading yet.

Trust that it is. Trust that your freedom matters. Trust that living with a little more ease, a little more release, a little more honesty changes not just you but everyone you touch.

That's the real transformation. Not becoming someone different. Just becoming more honestly yourself.

And letting that be enough.

CONCLUSION: The View From the Summit

I'm writing this from my grandmother's porch. The same porch where she found me three years ago, sitting on the floor of my closet, having an identity crisis because I didn't know who I was without my performance of who I thought I should be.

She's inside making coffee. I can hear her humming, the same song she's hummed my entire life, something her mother taught her in Spanish that she never translated for me. She doesn't need to. The melody says everything: this is home. You're safe here. Everything is exactly as it should be.

I came here this weekend because I wanted to write this conclusion somewhere that mattered. Not in my apartment where I've spent countless hours trying to manifest and visualize and force my life into alignment. But here, where the wisdom that changed everything was first offered to me at 2 AM over the phone when I was sobbing in a parking lot.

"Are you manifesting what you want," she'd asked me that night, "or what you think you're supposed to want?"

That question cracked me open. And what's poured out since then has been three years of slowly learning to live differently. To release instead of grip. To allow instead of force. To trust instead of control.

What I Know Now

If I could go back and talk to the version of me who was sitting in that car three years ago, mascara running, hyperventilating, achievement unlocked but happiness completely absent, here's what I would tell her:

You're not broken. You never were. You just forgot that you're allowed to want what you actually want instead of what you think impressive people want.

The trying is the problem. Not the solution. Every time you try harder to manifest, to force, to control, you're moving further from what you actually need, which is to stop trying and start being.

Your body knows things your mind doesn't. Stop overriding it with affirmations and visualizations and positive thinking. Start listening to it. The tightness in your chest is information. The exhaustion isn't laziness. The resistance isn't a block to clear, it's wisdom trying to get your attention.

Letting go isn't giving up. This is the hardest one to understand. But letting go of how it has to happen, when it has to happen, who has to be involved, that's not quitting. That's creating space for something better than you can currently imagine.

The grip will return. You're not going to transcend being human. You're going to keep falling back into old patterns. The difference is you'll notice faster, release easier, and have way more compassion for yourself in the process.

Your freedom is contagious. When you stop performing and start being real, you give everyone around you permission to do the same. You don't have to teach anyone anything. Just live differently. That's enough.

But I can't go back and tell her these things. She has to learn them the way I did, slowly, imperfectly, through a thousand small moments of choosing release over grip.

The Path You Just Walked

Look at where you started. Look at where you are now.

When you picked up this book, you were probably exhausted. Tired of trying so hard. Tired of all the manifestation practices that weren't working. Tired of the constant self-improvement that never felt like enough. Tired of living in the gap between who you are and who you think you should be.

Maybe you were skeptical. "Another self-help book telling me what's wrong with me and how to fix it." I don't blame you. I was skeptical too. Of everything. Especially of anything that promised answers.

But this book didn't promise to fix you. It promised something else: permission to stop trying to fix yourself. Permission to release the grip. Permission to be imperfectly, messily, beautifully human.

And if you've read this far, if you've done any of the practices, sat with any of the questions, noticed any of the patterns in your own life, something has already shifted.

Maybe it's small. Maybe you just noticed once this week that you were gripping and you released, just a little. Maybe you checked in with your body instead of overriding it. Maybe you said no to something you would have forced yourself through before.

That shift? That's everything. That's the whole work. Not some massive transformation that happens all at once. Just small moments of choosing differently, accumulating over time until one day you wake up and realize you're living an entirely different life.

What Happens Next

I'm not going to lie to you and say everything gets easy now. That if you just practice letting go, your life will become a highlight reel of manifestation wins and spiritual alignment.

Some things will get easier. You'll grip less. Force less. Suffer less from your own desperate need to control everything.

But life will still be life. Hard things will happen. You'll still face challenges, losses, disappointments. The difference is you won't make them worse by adding your own suffering on top of the natural difficulty.

Pain is inevitable. Suffering, the extra layer we add by resisting what is, by demanding reality be different, by beating ourselves up for not being further along, that's optional.

And you're learning to put that optional suffering down.

Here's what I think happens next for you:

You'll forget and remember. You'll forget to release and find yourself gripping again. Then you'll remember. This cycle will repeat forever. That's okay. That's the practice.

You'll get faster at noticing. Right now, you might grip for weeks before catching yourself. Soon it'll be days. Then hours. Then minutes. You'll still grip, but you'll return to release more quickly.

You'll trust yourself more. Not because you'll always make perfect decisions, but because you'll trust yourself to handle imperfect outcomes. That trust changes everything.

Your relationships will shift. Some people won't like the version of you who's stopped performing and people-pleasing. That's painful. But the relationships that remain will be so much richer because they're built on who you actually are.

Unexpected gifts will arrive. Not because you manifested them correctly, but because you finally created space for them. When your hands aren't clenched around what you think you need, they're open to receive what's actually trying to reach you.

You'll become boring in the best way. Less drama. Less crisis. More peace. More ordinary joy. Your Instagram might get less interesting. Your actual life will get infinitely better.

You'll stop waiting for someday. You'll start living now. Not because everything is perfect now, but because you've finally understood that this, right here, right now, exactly as you are, is where your life is actually happening.

The Letter I'm Not Sending

There's a letter I wrote to my father about six months ago. I haven't sent it. I probably never will. But writing it was part of my release practice, so I want to share part of it with you:

Dad,

I forgive you. Not because you've earned it or asked for it or even because you deserve it. I forgive you because I'm tired of carrying you with me everywhere I go.

For thirty years, I've organized my entire life around the fact that you left. Every relationship was filtered through "will this person leave too?" Every achievement was an attempt to prove I was worth staying for. Every moment of happiness was contaminated by waiting for it to end.

I made myself unlovable trying to become someone you'd come back for. I made myself exhausted trying to be so good, so perfect, so worthy that no one would ever leave me again.

I'm done.

I'm putting you down. Not because I've stopped loving you or stopped wishing you'd been different. But because I finally love myself more than I hate what you did.

You missed out on an incredible daughter. That's on you. But I don't have to miss out on my own life anymore.

I'm letting you go. And in letting you go, I'm finally free.

I cried for two hours after writing that letter. Then I felt something I'd never felt before: light. Untethered. Free.

That's what release actually does. It doesn't erase the past. It doesn't make the hurt okay. It just stops giving it power over your present.

What I Wish Someone Had Told Me

When I was deep in my manifestation obsession, desperate for answers, trying so hard to do everything right, I wish someone had told me:

The hardest part isn't learning to let go. It's giving yourself permission to let go.

You already know how. Somewhere in your body, you know exactly what release feels like. You've felt it before, maybe as a child, before you learned to grip. Maybe in rare moments of true presence.

The knowing is already there. You're just waiting for permission.

So here it is, written down, official, from someone who's walked this path before you:

You have permission to stop trying so hard.

You have permission to want what you actually want instead of what looks impressive.

You have permission to rest without earning it first.

You have permission to say no without a good excuse.

You have permission to quit things that aren't working.

You have permission to be exactly where you are instead of where you think you should be by now.

You have permission to be messy and imperfect and still worthy of love.

You have permission to let go.

Not someday, when you've finally healed enough or worked hard enough or proven yourself enough. Right now. Today. This moment.

You have permission.

The Practice I Still Come Back To

On hard days, when I catch myself gripping again, when old patterns resurface, when I forget everything I've learned and find myself desperately trying to force outcomes, I come back to one simple practice.

I close my eyes. I imagine I'm holding whatever I'm clutching in my clenched fists.

Then I slowly open my hands. Turn my palms up. And I say out loud:

"I release my grip on this. I trust that whatever is meant to stay will stay. Whatever is meant to go can go. I am safe in the releasing."

Sometimes I have to do this seventeen times in one day. Sometimes I forget for weeks and then remember when I'm wound so tight I can barely breathe.

The practice isn't perfect. I'm not perfect. But it works. Not because it's magic, but because it reminds my body of what my mind keeps forgetting: I don't have to hold on so tight. I'm safe in the letting go.

Try it now. Whatever you're gripping, whether you know what it is or not, just imagine releasing it. Opening your hands. Turning your palms up.

Feel that sensation in your body. That's what freedom feels like.

My Grandmother's Wisdom

My grandmother just brought me coffee. She sat down next to me on the porch swing, and we swung in silence for a while, the way we do.

"How's the book coming?" she finally asked.

"It's done. I'm writing the conclusion."

"What are you telling them?"

I thought about it. "I'm telling them what you told me. That letting go isn't the same as giving up. That they don't have to try so hard. That they're allowed to just be."

She smiled. "Good. That's what they need to hear."

"How did you know?" I asked. "How did you always know?"

She was quiet for a long moment. Then: "Because I spent the first half of my life gripping, mija. Trying to control everything. Forcing outcomes. Making myself sick with the effort of holding my life together through sheer will."

This surprised me. I'd always seen her as this wise, peaceful woman who had it all figured out.

"What changed?" I asked.

"I got tired. So tired I couldn't do it anymore. And when I stopped, when I finally just let everything be what it was going to be, I discovered that life doesn't fall apart when you stop holding it together. It actually starts flowing."

She paused. "The tomatoes taught me that."

We both laughed. The damn tomatoes. Her perennial wisdom-delivery system.

"Everything I needed to know about life," she said, "I learned from gardening. You can't force a seed to grow faster. You can't control the weather. You can't make the harvest come on your timeline. All you can do is plant, water, trust. The rest is up to forces bigger than you."

"And that's enough?" I asked.

"That's everything," she said.

The View From Here

The title of this conclusion is "The View From the Summit." But I want to be clear about something: this isn't the top. There is no top.

You don't climb this mountain and arrive at a peak where everything is perfect and complete and you've got it all figured out. You don't graduate from the school of letting go.

The summit metaphor is wrong. This is more like learning to surf. You don't catch one perfect wave and then you're done. You keep catching waves. Some you ride beautifully. Some knock you over. Some you miss completely.

The ocean keeps coming. The waves keep arriving. And you keep practicing. Getting better, sure. Falling less often, probably. But still practicing. Still learning. Still in relationship with forces bigger than you.

That's the view from here: not that I've arrived, but that I've stopped needing to arrive. Not that I've figured it all out, but that I've made peace with not having it figured out.

I still have goals. Still have dreams. Still move toward things I want.

But I'm not gripping them anymore. I'm holding them lightly. Dancing with them instead of wrestling them to the ground.

And from here, from this place of open-handed living, I can see so much more than I could when I was desperately focused on forcing one specific outcome.

I can see opportunities I would have missed because they didn't match my plan. I can see people I would have overlooked because they didn't fit my list. I can see possibilities I couldn't have imagined when I was clutching one narrow vision of how life had to unfold.

The view from here is vast. Open. Full of more possibility than my old clenched-fist life could ever hold.

What I Hope For You

As this book comes to a close, here's what I hope for you:

I hope you practice release. Not perfectly. Not all at once. Just small moments of opening your hands instead of clenching your fists.

I hope you notice when you're gripping and have compassion for yourself instead of shame.

I hope you trust your body's wisdom more than any guru's blueprint.

I hope you let go of timelines that aren't serving you and trust that your life is unfolding exactly as it needs to.

I hope you forgive, not everyone, not perfectly, but whoever you're ready to release because carrying them is exhausting.

I hope you stop performing and start being. Stop curating and start living. Stop waiting for someday and start showing up for today.

I hope you find your own version of the ceramics class, the tomato garden, the wise grandmother, the 2 AM phone call that cracks you open and lets the truth in.

I hope you learn to want without needing, to plan without clutching, to dream without demanding.

I hope you discover that you're so much more magnetic when you're being yourself than when you're trying to be impressive.

I hope you fall back into gripping a thousand times and come back to release a thousand and one.

I hope your freedom becomes medicine for others without you even trying.

Most of all, I hope you're kind to yourself through all of it. This isn't about doing it right. It's about doing it at all.

The Beginning

My grandmother is calling me in for breakfast. Real breakfast, eggs and beans and tortillas, not a "high-vibration" smoothie I don't actually want.

Before I go, I want to leave you with this:

This isn't the end of the book. It's the beginning of your practice.

Everything you've read here is just words on pages until you live it. Until you try it. Until you mess it up and try again.

The real work starts now. Not someday when you feel ready. Not when you've healed enough or understood enough or become enough.

Now. Today. This imperfect moment.

You already have everything you need. You don't need another course, another teacher, another technique. You just need to practice opening your hands.

Start small. One release. One moment of choosing allow instead of force. One breath of "what if I didn't have to control this?"

That's enough. That's everything.

The path of release isn't about arriving anywhere. It's about walking differently right now, wherever you are.

So walk. Stumble. Fall. Get back up. Walk some more.

And know that somewhere, maybe on a porch in the morning sun, maybe drinking coffee with my grandmother, maybe writing the next chapter of my own imperfect life, I'm walking too.

We're doing this together. Messily. Imperfectly. Humanly.

With open hands and full hearts and the courage to keep letting go.

Welcome to the rest of your life.

It starts now.

APPENDIX A: The Quick Release Guide

Emergency Tools for When You're Spiraling

You're in the bathroom at work, trying not to cry. Or lying in bed at 3 AM, chest tight with anxiety. Or sitting in your car after a hard day, paralyzed by overwhelm.

You need help now. Not a deep practice. Not a long meditation. Just something to get you from drowning to breathing.

Here are the emergency tools. Use what works. Leave the rest.

The 60-Second Body Reset

When you're spiraling, you're in your head. These get you back in your body fast.

The Shake
Stand up. Shake your hands vigorously for 10 seconds. Like you're shaking off water. Then shake your whole body. Let yourself look ridiculous. This discharges stuck energy faster than anything I know.

The Squeeze and Release
Clench every muscle in your body as tight as you can. Hold for 5 seconds. Then release everything at once. Repeat 3 times. This teaches your nervous system the difference between grip and release.

The Ground
Take off your shoes. Put your feet flat on the floor. Press down like you're trying to push through the floor. Feel the solid ground beneath you. Say out loud: "I am here. I am safe. This will pass."

The Emergency Breath Pattern

Your breath is the fastest way to shift your nervous system. But NOT deep breathing when you're activated, that can make it worse.

The 4-7-8 Breath
Breathe in through your nose for 4 counts.
Hold for 7 counts.
Exhale through your mouth for 8 counts.
Repeat 4 times.

The long exhale signals your vagus nerve that you're safe. It's biology, not woo-woo.

The Spiral Stoppers

When your mind is spinning in worst-case scenarios:

The 5-4-3-2-1
Name out loud:
5 things you can see
4 things you can touch
3 things you can hear
2 things you can smell
1 thing you can taste

This pulls you out of your catastrophizing mind and into present-moment sensation.

The Reality Check
Ask yourself three questions:

1. Am I in immediate physical danger right now? (Usually the answer is no.)
2. What's actually happening versus what I'm afraid might happen?
3. Have I survived 100% of my worst days so far?

Write down the answers if you can.

The Emergency Releases

The Dump
Grab paper and pen. Write every single thing in your head. Don't edit. Don't make it make sense. Just dump it all out. Then rip it up or throw it away. The physical act of throwing it away helps your brain let it go.

The Permission Slip
Write yourself a permission slip. Literally. "I, [your name], give myself permission to not have this figured out right now. I give myself permission to be a mess. I give myself permission to need help."

Sign it. Keep it somewhere you can see it.

The Future Self Letter
Write a letter from your future self, the version of you who's on the other side of this crisis, to your current self. What would they tell you? Usually something like: "You get through this. I know because I'm you and I'm here. You're stronger than you think."

The Physical Releases

Sometimes you need to move energy through your body, not just your mind.

The Cry

If you need to cry, cry. Don't hold it in. Don't try to "shift your vibration." Tears are how your body releases stress hormones. Let them flow.

The Scream

If you can find privacy (car, pillow, shower), scream. Let the sound come from your belly. Release everything you're holding in your throat.

The Walk

If you can move, walk. Not exercise, just walk. Let your body move rhythmically. No destination. No goal. Just movement.

The Emergency Mantra

When nothing else is working, repeat this:

"This feeling is temporary. I've felt this before and it passed. It will pass again. I am safe in this moment, even though I'm uncomfortable."

Say it out loud if you can. Over and over until your nervous system starts to believe it.

What NOT to Do

When you're spiraling, your instinct might be to:

- Immediately try to fix the problem
- Force yourself to think positive
- Beat yourself up for being a mess

- Reach for numbing (scroll, drink, shop, whatever your version is)

Don't. These make it worse.

Instead: Just survive the next 5 minutes. Then the next 5 minutes. Then the next.

You don't have to fix anything right now. You just have to get through this moment.

And you will. Because you always have.

APPENDIX B: Recommended Reading & Resources

Books That Helped Me Release

On Letting Go:

- *Letting Go: The Pathway of Surrender* by David R. Hawkins
- *The Untethered Soul* by Michael Singer
- *Radical Acceptance* by Tara Brach

On Nervous System Healing:

- *The Body Keeps the Score* by Bessel van der Kolk
- *Waking the Tiger* by Peter Levine

- *Polyvagal Theory in Therapy* by Deb Dana

On Being Human:

- *The Gifts of Imperfection* by Brené Brown
- *When Things Fall Apart* by Pema Chödrön
- *The Wisdom of No Escape* by Pema Chödrön

On Different Approaches to Manifestation:

- *The Big Leap* by Gay Hendricks (on upper limit problems)
- *The Mountain Is You* by Brianna Wiest (on self-sabotage)
- *Breaking the Habit of Being Yourself* by Dr. Joe Dispenza

Teachers & Resources

Somatic Practices:

- Irene Lyon (nervous system work)
- Peter Levine (somatic experiencing)
- The Embody Lab (trauma-informed movement)

Mindfulness Without the Spiritual Bypass:

- Jon Kabat-Zinn (MBSR - secular mindfulness)
- Tara Brach (compassionate awareness)
- Jack Kornfield (wise heart practices)

On Attachment & Relationships:

- Attached by Amir Levine & Rachel Heller
- Polysecure by Jessica Fern
- Hold Me Tight by Dr. Sue Johnson

Apps & Tools (The Helpful Ones)

Insight Timer - Free meditation app without the toxic positivity
Dare - For anxiety, based in neuroscience not manifestation
Finch - Self-care app that doesn't shame you

What I Don't Recommend

I'm not going to list these specifically, but be cautious of:

- Anything promising manifestation in X days
- Teachers who blame you for everything that goes wrong
- Programs that cost thousands and promise miraculous results
- Anyone who makes you feel broken or not spiritual enough
- Content that makes you feel worse about yourself

Trust your gut. If something feels manipulative or shame-based, it probably is.

ACKNOWLEDGMENTS

To my grandmother, Maria: You answered the phone at 2 AM and changed my life with one question. Everything in this book comes back to your wisdom. Thank you for loving me through the beautiful prison I built and celebrating with me when I finally walked out. Your tomatoes are still the best teachers I've ever had.

To Christine: Thank you for being the therapist who didn't try to fix me, who saw my coping mechanisms as wisdom instead of pathology, and who gave me permission to be a mess while I figured my shit out. The "worthiness archaeology" changed everything.

To Rachel: For being the friend who told me hard truths I needed to hear. For not abandoning me when I was in my worst manifestation obsession phase. For noticing when I started to change and reflecting back to me what I couldn't see yet in myself.

To Diane: My ceramics teacher who taught me more about life than about pottery. "You can't force the clay" became my mantra. Thank you for creating space for me to fall apart and remake myself, literally and figuratively.

To Marcus: For loving the real me instead of the performed version. For not needing me to be healed before you chose me. For showing me what wholeness looks like in relationship. For reading terrible early drafts of this book and still believing in it.

To my father: I forgive you. This acknowledgment doesn't mean I'm excusing what you did. It means I'm finally free from what it did to me.

To Jessica, Maya, Alex, Lisa, and all the friends who let me practice release in real relationships: Thank you for staying when I stopped performing, for calling me out when I was full of shit, and for celebrating the small shifts that eventually became transformation.

To every person in my grief group, my ceramics class, my manifestation courses, my therapy waiting rooms: Your shared humanity made me feel less alone. Your stories are woven through mine, even when I changed the names and details. Thank you for letting your struggles be seen.

To the manifestation teachers I eventually disagreed with: I'm grateful for what you taught me, even as I've moved beyond it. You gave me tools that worked until they didn't. That's not a failure on your part, that's growth on mine.

To everyone who's ever told me I was "too much" or "not enough": Thank you for the pain that taught me I don't need everyone's approval to live my life.

To you, reading this: Thank you for trusting me with your time and attention. For being willing to question everything you've been taught about manifestation and success and worthiness. For practicing release even when it's hard. You're braver than you think.

Printed in Dunstable, United Kingdom

77802756R00143